About Our Schools

ALEC CLEGG

About Our Schools

BASIL BLACKWELL · OXFORD

© Sir Alec Clegg 1980

First published in 1980 by
Basil Blackwell Publisher
108 Cowley Rd,
Oxford,
OX4 1JF

British Library Cataloguing in Publication Data
Clegg, *Sir* Alec
　　About Our Schools.
　　1. Education — Great Britain
　　I. Title
　　370'.941　　　LA632
　　ISBN 0–631–12881–6
　　ISBN 0–631–12832–8　Pbk

Typeset by Oxford Publishing Services
Printed in Great Britain by
Billing and Sons Ltd
Guildford, London, Oxford, Worcester

Contents

Chapter 15 is reprinted here by kind permission of the Controller of Her Majesty's Stationery Office.

Introduction

In the years that have passed since the Education Act of 1944 established for the first time in this country a coherent system of primary, secondary and further education, all those concerned with the schools have been drenched with books, reports, pamphlets and theses telling them what they should do and how and why they should do it. Anyone adding to the flood is likely to be asked what made him presume so to do and what are his qualifications for doing it.

It is with uncomfortable diffidence that I attempt to answer these questions. I suppose my main justification for writing is that for almost the whole of the thirty-year period of exuberant recuperation and development which followed the last war, I was the education officer of one of the biggest and most diverse authorities in the country, and for those of us who were education officers in those days, it was a golden era. Education was going to put the world to rights; and in the twenty years from 1954 to 1974 something like half the schools in the area which I served were either newly built or rebuilt. We sent students to the universities and into other forms of further education in vastly increased numbers, and the annual expenditure in the authority for which I worked rose over this thirty-year span from some £7 million or so, to well over £100 million. Moreover we saw something like a revolution in our primary schools and the advent of comprehensive schools at the secondary stage. It was the period of the great reports.

Crowther (1959) looked at the schooling of youngsters of fifteen to eighteen years of age, Newsom (1963) at the slow learners of thirteen to sixteen, Plowden (1967) at children in their primary schools, and Robbins (1963) at the universities, and there were also the massive researches of the National Children's Bureau, the National Foundation for Educational Research, and of many other competent and effective workers.

My interest in all these happenings was stimulated and sustained by my own experience. I was educated in a dame school and a State County Secondary School, and later at an independent boarding school.

I lived for six months with an elderly man and his wife who directed a girls' finishing school in Weimar. After taking my degree and my teaching certificate, I taught for four years at a London aided grammar school. Apart from the sojourn in the girls' boarding school, there was nothing unusual in what I did, but times were hard, and when I began to teach in 1932 many of us who had trained together failed to get immediate employment, and when we got it our salaries were cut by 10 per cent.

As time passed, however, there were other unusual elements in my experience which gave me interest and support. The first was that my grandfather, my father and I between us had covered the education service since it began. My grandfather became an elementary-school headmaster in 1869, the year before the service was founded. My father became a secondary-school head following the 1902 Act which first permitted us to spend money on secondary schools, and I was appointed as Chief Officer in the West Riding of Yorkshire in 1945, the year after the service was made complete by the 1944 Act. This family record was by no means unique, but I suspect that my succession of administrative appointments was. By some strange twist of chance, I became the first Administrative Assistant to be appointed by the Birmingham Authority, the first Assistant for Higher Education to be appointed by the Cheshire Authority, the first Deputy Education Officer in Worcestershire and the first Deputy in the West Riding.

But my learning about education owed much to two groups of people. The first was my immediate family and their wives and husbands, as between us in one way or another we had experienced almost every kind of educational position from a reception class teacher to the principal of a university college, from a teacher in a direct-grant school to the vice-chairman of the governors of a school for disruptive girls, from a teacher in a technical college to an HMI. I gained further intimate and personal experience from the fact that one of my sisters who died at the age of sixty-two years never developed intellectually beyond the age of six or seven. My three sons all attended the first comprehensive school to be established in the West Riding, as it was the school which served their home.

The second group from which I learned was made up of a number of colleagues and teachers with whom I worked when I first began in the West Riding. They taught me my job, and they did it by showing me quality and achievement in the schools which were beyond question. It is this quality of work, and what promotes and inhibits it, that has moved me to write.

I shall of course make no attempt to produce a thesis based on educational theory, as I have neither the knowledge, the scholarship nor the ability to attempt such a task. Neither shall I attempt to write about those areas of which I have had relatively little personal experience; I refer for instance to the whole range of further education, to our special schools for the handicapped, to our school meals service. These and other sections of the service were dealt with directly by my Deputy and other colleagues, and it would be somewhat dishonest of me to give the impression I was in any way deeply knowledgeable about them.

But I have visited and still do visit many schools that have managed to overcome stupendous difficulties. Despite all that is against them, they nourish their children in mind, body and spirit in ways which never cease to excite my deep admiration and indeed my wonder.

I have written a personal, almost an autobiographical

account of my experiences as an education officer as this has enabled me more effectively to reveal the debts that I owe to the teachers, advisers and office colleagues with whom I have worked.

My hope is that what I have written may prove of some value to all who are concerned with the well-being of our education service, be they students about to study it, teachers who have to withstand its buffetings, officials who administer it, or parents who want to get the most out of it for their children.

PART I

Attitudes and Practice

1

Schools which Changed my Views

When I began as an education administrator the elementary-school pattern of working was fairly clearly established in my mind. At 9 o'clock children were lined up in the playground and marched into their classrooms. After the register had been called to find out who was absent or late, they were marched into the hall to take part in the assembly which consisted of a hymn and a prayer followed by notices. Once back in the classrooms the day's work began with scripture, followed by arithmetic and the other traditional subjects according to the timetable, which had to be fixed in a prominent place so that the visiting Inspector could readily see it. The lessons which were given were expected to conform to the scheme of work which the class teacher had prepared at the beginning of the term and handed to the head teacher.

Arithmetic was divided into 'mental, mechanical and problems'. Multiplication tables were chanted and the intricacies of the four rules thoroughly practised and the well-known shopping and bath-filling sums worked out.

History began with the Ancient Britons and proceeded story by story through the centuries; geography and even nature study were taught from 'efficient' books. English consisted of compositions on a theme chosen by the teacher using words set out on the blackboard, and there were of course also the well-known exercises in dictation, comprehension and grammar. The teacher taught the children how to draw and paint objects, and craft for the girls consisted of the hemming, gathering and seaming of garments, and for the boys bookbinding.

As the 11 plus examination assumed more and more influence it exerted more and more control. The old exam, which used to consist of papers in English composition and arithmetic, gave place to standardized tests in these subjects supported by a standardized intelligent test, and 'intelligence' as a subject crept into the timetable. As all this went on the pupils were grouped into the clever, the average and the dull. The clever ones at the top of the class filled the two rows on the right of the teacher as he faced them, those at the bottom were on the extreme left, and the middling ones were in the middle. Children changed places continually as they moved up and down, but those at the top tended to stay at the top while those at the bottom seldom rose.

The main feature of this organization was that whatever was taught could be given a mark and the children were graded accordingly. The clever children were given the spur of recognition and praise which the dull were denied on the grounds that they seldom deserved it, as all too often they were merely lazy. Moreover, if they were dull the sooner they were made to face up to it the better.

There was of course punishment as well as praise and reward. I so well remember that when I was a student in training at the London Day Training College I had to see some elementary-school work and was sent to a school in Hotham Road, Putney. The real day began with twenty mental arithmetic questions put to the class at what seemed to me to be great speed. Papers were exchanged by the pupils and corrected with equal speed. Those with less than five correct answers did not wait to be summoned, they walked to the front, held out their hands and took one stroke of the cane. The embar-

rassing aspect of all this as far as I was concerned was that had
they but known it I should have had to hold out my hand, for
despite my BA I could rarely have secured six correct answers
in the allotted time. Once started, the day went on with its
memorizing and its testing of arduously acquired skills, subjects were drilled into the children and the teacher knew precisely how to drive home the technical tricks by which each
skill was mastered. And I saw nothing wrong in this — it was
eminently sensible. The teachers were more often than not
kindly, considerate folk. Children were graded according to
their ability, teachers knew precisely what they had to teach
throughout the year, the three Rs had to be mastered and a
body of information in each timetabled subject had to be
learned.

Behaviour problems had similarly to be dealt with by accepted techniques. Children were good, middling and bad, and
the bad had to be caned into submission if they misbehaved or
broke the clearly understood rules. In matters of this kind
scripture was important because it improved the children's
morals. Obedience was important and 'because I say so' was a
good enough reason for the teacher to give to the child.

It was this pattern of elementary schooling that I took to my
first administrative post in the City of Birmingham, and it was
there that I got my first suspicion that perhaps my pattern was
in some instances somewhat limited. I knew little of the nursery-
school world, though as a student at Cambridge I had heard
odd things about a school near where my married sister lived,
called the Malting House School, run by one Susan Isaacs. But
as a young administrator I was concerned with more serious
matters such as the 11 plus. However, one day a local Birmingham Inspector took me into a school in Steward Street
which seemed one of the markedly poorer areas of the city. As
we entered, my worry developed. There was no sign of a
teacher, but children were kneeling on the cloakroom floor
surrounded by wet coats hanging on the pegs and they were
painting. Inside the hall of the school a similar group was
acting. I found the whole visit extremely embarrassing and

wondered what good all this did to their preparation for the 11 plus. There was however one aspect of what I saw which puzzled me. There was no teacher with the children who were painting with their paper on the cloakroom floor and they were so engrossed in what they were doing that they paid no attention whatever to the Inspector or to me. This same absorption was equally noticeable in the acting going on in the hall. How, I wondered, did they get that degree of concentration, but I managed to dismiss this puzzle from my mind and to pay attention to what I believed were more serious matters. But when some years after I had moved to Worcestershire the Authority for some reason which I only vaguely understood wanted to appoint a Drama Adviser, I gave my support to the Steward Street head, Mr A. R. Stone. He was appointed and later moved with me to the West Riding and as time passed he taught me more about primary-school work than anyone else. He wrote a very valuable booklet which was published by the Stationery Office. It was entitled *The Story of a School*.

Also in Worcestershire I met Diana Jordan, an eminent disciple of Rudolf Laban who had come to this country as a fugitive from Hitler. Laban's expertise was in the study of movement, be it in connection with dance, drama or physical education generally. I had seen Diana Jordan teaching the Girls' Training Corps in Laban's ways and was again bewildered and profoundly moved by the fact that all were utterly absorbed in what they were doing. No one seemed in any way ill at ease, no matter how ungainly or unskilled she might appear to be, and again none was disturbed by the intrusion of visitors.

At that time I also became vaguely aware of the existence of Cizek, a Viennese teacher of the young, who apparently believed that every child could draw and paint. I did not for one moment believe this but when I moved to the West Riding I was made to hesitate. We appointed a painter of some distinction, Basil Rocke, as our Art Adviser. He had worked with Cizek in Vienna. At the same time we appointed as his assistant Ruth Scrivener who, when she was a teacher at

Bedales, had taught the children who produced much of the work which illustrated Herbert Read's book *Education Through Art*.

These two people, together with Laban whom I had met, and Diana Jordan, made me doubt my own beliefs about traditional primary-school methods. I remembered my Steward Street experience but took comfort in the fact that this was only one school and so by and large I stuck to my views. After all, I knew little of Susan Isaacs or the Macmillan sisters or Bertrand Russell or Dewey or Neill, and my mind clung to the principle, 'This is what you have to do, this is how you have to do it, do it or else.' But a West Riding vacation course held in 1948 introduced me to new theories and practices. The people who attended it, many of whom had just come back from the army, were not told how to teach children to paint; they themselves had to paint. As with art so with movement. They were taught not how to move according to a prescribed pattern, but in a way which was for them the best way of mastering the objective. I was doubtful about the whole thing, but I could not rid myself of the nagging suspicion that there might be something in it, especially when I thought back to the intense and utter absorption of the young children at Steward Street School and the older ones at the Girls' Training Corps in Evesham. There followed other experiences which began inevitably to make me think that there might be newer and different ways of teaching and that Laban and Cizek might be right.

There were about a thousand primary schools in the West Riding in those days and many of them were serving the coalfields which consisted of many small closely-knit and powerful communities, housed often in deplorable back-to-back dwellings. The children attended schools which were housed in old buildings, but were often of the central hall type which had much to commend it. In such schools most of the children were the sons and daughters of coal miners and only a very small proportion were born of middle-class families. Amidst these village communities were the small towns, such as Castleford, Mexborough and Featherstone, where the social life centred round the pit, the brass band and the rugby league club.

In his book *Yorkshire: The West Riding* (1959) Nikolaus Pevsner said of Castleford: 'There does not seem to be a single building in the centre of the town which would justify mention.' But he made an exception of Oliver Hill's Infant School, and I well remember my early visits to that school. It was under the direction of Miss Mary Walker and I recall how surprised I was to see small six-year-olds wielding saws and hammers, nails and other dangerous instruments while others painted, wrote, read, measured, weighed and shopped. I knew something of what infants did for when in Birmingham I had had the good fortune to marry the teacher of one of their best reception classes, but in these later years Whitwood Mere went beyond anything I had previously seen. I was bewildered and impressed by its order which I believed owed much to the newness of the building.

An Inspector colleague of mine, however, cast some doubt on this view by taking me to an old but well-kept colourful building set amidst the colliery houses in Regent Street, Featherstone, where another Miss Walker, Miss Marjorie Walker, was doing work which I found equally astonishing. In both these schools the children found so much joy that they arrived early in the morning and stayed as long as they could after school had finished. I remember taking the Minister of Education to this school. We stood in the playground for a time at about 8.45 a.m. watching the last of the parents bringing their five and six-year-olds into the school. Many parents went into the school with the children but few seemed to come out. At about 9 o'clock Lord Boyle and I walked into the school and by this time the parents were coming out, but to our astonishment there seemed to be no teachers about. However, each child was in his place, busily engaged in the work carefully put out the evening before by the teacher who knew what every child was doing. I remember a triumph which I enjoyed at this same school. Mr Mander Jones, the Director

General of Education for South Australia, paid us a visit and I decided to take him to the Featherstone school. We went in as the school began and the children were engaged in activities of all kinds. My Australian friend had obvious doubts about what he was seeing. He went to the book corner and chose what for such small children was a most difficult book. He then beckoned to the most unlikely looking boy in the room. As Mander Jones opened the book my heart sank. But when the boy was asked to read, he did so well that the impression made on the visitor was as deep as the relief which I felt.

But in those early years I had doubts not unlike those of my Australian guest. I could not deny the quality of what I had seen at Regent Street and Whitwood Mere, even though I had not seen similar quality elsewhere. Neither could I deny the principles on which the two heads worked, which were that children do best what they enjoy doing; that because of their varying rates of development they should, as far as possible, be taught as individuals; that they should experience and understand the need for drills and techniques before they are called upon to master them; that they should not be given all they want but should have all that they need to enable them to learn; and so on. In what these schools were doing HMI supported them vigorously and extolled their virtues in written reports.

But, I said to myself, these were after all infant schools; one could not use methods and approaches of this kind with children in junior schools. However, a handful of our junior schools began to provide evidence that neither I nor anyone else could deny, and yet again a number of incidents forced me to change my views.

One day as I was at work in my office one of our County Council Inspectors brought in some children's paintings for me to see. They came from a sad old wooden school in the grim mining village of Thurnscoe. I was astonished by their quality and maturity and made enquiries about what was happening in the school. I discovered that the Assistant Art Adviser had visited the school and had sought to encourage the staff to give more initiative to the children rather than telling them what to do. She had met with a rebuff. Their job, so the teachers said, was to teach children what to do and how to do it. However, the headmaster himself, Mr Frank Jones, had been moved by his experience at the vacation course where he had had to paint, and once back in his own school he undertook some class teaching with such success that the excitement rapidly spread throughout the school with unexpected results. For instance, I was informed by an Adviser, Miss Jordan, in whom I had complete trust, that side by side with the vast improvement in painting, there had been other developments. Children were writing far more than they had written before and scores of them were working unsupervised throughout the dinner hour. Moreover there was a freshness and imagination about the written work which was new. There seemed to be a direct connection between the satisfaction and recognition that the children were getting for their successful painting, and the quality of their written work. Her note was as follows:

The 'progress' of this school in the new approach is steady. The 'art' side still leads and flowers even more fully each term. I think that the art is really the best I have ever seen or imagined from a junior school. But the result of the whole philosophy in practice is that this interest and learning process so evident in the art is beginning to affect the academic side. I have not had the opportunity to investigate this fully this term so do not wish to say more, and Mr Armstrong (our Educational Psychologist) is now following up his introduction to the school and, I gather, is amazed.

But one practical problem is arising, i.e. adequate provision of materials. This is affected in one or two ways and I quote an example or two:
(1) The development of the art rests upon sufficient paper and art materials, and, since every child is pouring out his ideas boldly and increasingly, naturally there is more and more demand. In addition, on wet days in the dinner hour there have been as many as 180 children found in the classrooms working unsupervised, seriously and fully absorbed in painting, modelling, writing and reading. (This has necessitated having the materials available to them and has been neatly organized. It is to be noted that there is no waste of materials, owing to the children's control.)

(2) Composition books: Whereas a child took 18 months to fill a composition book, they now in some cases use as many as 1½ books a term. I am sending you this evidence with notes on the 'cases'. When you look at the books you will see what I mean. The awakened imagination and freed expression is beginning to produce a flow of language that cannot be stopped. The requisition for exercise books is becoming a problem as are pens and pencils, besides art materials. This all being on capitation is about to produce a problem in this school. Mr Jones, the headmaster, has discussed it all with the divisional officer, Mr Stockdale, who is also very interested in the school. Mr Jones is now approximately £10 overdrawn on his capitation allowance with the spring term to go and the 'pinch' will come about March at the latest. He told me that two heads of schools had said they didn't know how they could spend the capitation allowance! It is thought to be very fair, not to say generous — but on the approach which Mr Jones is making and which we hope will spread, it is going to be a problem. He said he would be willing for me to tell you this as a matter of principle, and not as a complaint — a bare statement of a problem now very near to him. If you would like any particular evidence and facts will you let me know?

Again I took all this with bewildered doubt, but the fact that aroused me most was that since the new ways began, this tough school had been almost free from visits by the police and the probation officer. Moved as I was by this, I could not believe that all children were affected, and I tended to attribute the Thurnscoe success to the gifted teachers working with a group of exceptional children, an experience which many schools have lived through.

Then came another event. At Wheldon Lane School in a socially deprived area of Castleford, I went to see some extra-ordinary dramatic movement conducted by Miss Bessie Bullough. Again what moved me was the absorption of the children and their intense devotion to the job on hand, and this applied not only to the lithe and the gifted, but to the one or two who were developing with a certain physical grossness. I was deeply moved by this experience as were a group of young athletics teachers from Germany with whom I visited the school, not to mention the Minister of Education whom I had also taken to see what was going on. I recall that this particular work disturbed people because the response of the children had an intensity which was almost frightening. The sensitivity of the group was obviously very great. But it was the uninhibited and sensitive athletic endeavour of every single child that was equally astonishing. For the first time in my life I had seen a class where every child, apt or unapt, 'could do it' and every child enjoyed what was being done.

There followed another experience which made an equally deep impression on me. I went one day to a school in South Kirkby whose headmaster, Mr Gordon, had attended the same significant vacation course as that attended by Mr Jones of Thurnscoe, and Mrs Gordon was responsible for a class of ten-year-olds. Once more the first thing that struck me was that when I went into the class no teacher was present yet the children were wholly absorbed in painting with potentially dangerous material such as powder paint and water. The discipline was obviously of a very high order. But when I went into the hall there were pinned up at child height some thirty paintings of flowers, each with its own individuality and to me each possessed of extraordinary quality. Here again was such clear evidence that at last I was forced to accept that 'every child could do it'; that is every child could give intense personal expression of a high order and quality of something which had moved his spirit, and what I saw was not merely the result of technical instruction. I was by this time convinced that my colleagues were right and that although obviously some work showed much greater technical ability than other work, all the pieces on view were infused with deep feeling and were the result of intense personal effort. But again, as at Whitwood Mere, Thurnscoe and Wheldon Lane, what really impressed me was the discipline of the children which arose from the obvious fact that the teaching was pleasurably absorbing their surplus energies; it recognized their endeavour, it gave them success on which the teacher could continue to build.

I found other schools which had this same effect on me. The

village school in the coal-mining village of Rossington had been taken over by a new head, Mr Horner, who had come back from the war. He was a practised athlete but he took up Laban's teaching of movement and got more from his youngsters by its adoption than by any traditional methods he had previously used. He too found that by this movement training and the skilled use of craft he could arouse vitality in his pupils which had a profound effect not only on the school's expressive work but on the three Rs. This school eventually produced some of the most remarkable work I have seen.

Some time later I went back to a school at Castleford and saw the work of Mrs Muriel Pyrah, which I found quite baffling. It was unlike anything I had ever seen and indeed I have never seen its like. Mrs Pyrah had developed a technique of 'asking out'. At the beginning of the week her children, under her practised eye, prepared their work for the week and got on with it individually. Their teacher was available for talk and discussion about their problems, but the main teaching technique in this class was what was known to all as 'asking out'. It was the exact reverse of everything that I had ever been taught to do. The principle behind it was, if you don't know how, ask someone in the class who does, or ask the whole class. The result was that at any time when one visited the class some child or other would come out to the front of the class and ask about a problem that he was having to cope with at that moment, be it a mode of expression, a matter of fact, or merely a spelling. The effect of this technique was amazing. In the first place once the shyness had worn off 'asking out' became a recognized technique of learning. Furthermore, as most of the children in the class were born into families where acceptable school English was seldom used, one of the most beneficial aspects of this technique was that children had to ask for what they wanted in correct English, otherwise they would at once be put right by those of the class who were aware of the error. 'Asking out' in this way became a most powerful method of teaching correct English and, as every demand for a correct spelling had to be written on the blackboard, spelling too was of an abnormally high standard, and very soon most of the children achieved adult level in the standardized reading tests.

One of the most telling effects of this unusual technique of teaching was that children became extremely observant. Have I got the colour right? How could I give a better impression of distance just there? Is there a better word I could use? And so on. The total result of this constant process was that the children not only became severe critics themselves but accepted severe criticism, and their work became outstanding. I recall a number of incidents connected with this class. I was so bewildered by the technique of 'asking out' that I one day paused before going into the classroom to see if it happened with equal force when no visitor was present. It did; but I felt as if I had been listening at the keyhole and I confessed and apologized to Mrs Pyrah.

There were other incidents connected with her teaching. The first time I ever saw her with her class she told me she no longer used the lesson bell as it was obviously silly to make a child break off from a piece of work if he was deeply engrossed in it. Several years later I asked her if she knew what the 'integrated day' was and she confessed she had never heard of it, and I had to explain to her that I suspected that she had invented it. But her results were so exceptional that again doubts crept into mind. We still in those days used the 11 plus test and a vast majority of Mrs Pyrah's pupils secured an IQ of well over 100, which was obviously abnormal for such children. Moreover, of her thirty-two children twenty-eight qualified for grammar-school entrance rather than the eight or so which might have been expected. In the county at that time we used the Moray House tests and I was so suspicious of Mrs Pyrah's results that I went to the school myself armed with a set of National Foundation tests which I took care to see being worked and which were marked at my office. I was so surprised with the results that I sent them for comment to Sir Cyril Burt, my former teacher. He replied, making no observation on the fact that the passes were grossly in excess of anything which could be justified, but merely pointing out that the correlation between the two lists exceeded 90 per cent.

Again it was the discipline of the children which astonished me. I remember going into the class early one Monday morning only to find it without a teacher. By this time the class knew me and I them, and I asked them what they would do if Mrs Pyrah did not return. There was a silence and one child said, 'What do you mean?' I said, 'Well Mrs Pyrah isn't here now, suppose something happened which kept her away from you?' and there came from Sean Tiffany the immediate answer, 'We should get on.' I then said, 'Well how long would you get on for?' and received the astonishing reply, 'Until about Thursday.' 'Why Thursday?' I asked. 'Well,' said Sean, 'today is Monday, we've all prepared our work for the week and if some of us get through it before Friday I should think we might start larking about. That's why I said Thursday.'

The schools I have described and others like them forced me to change my views about junior-school work. In all of them, standards in the basic skills were high and standards in expressive work were abnormally so, and in all, behaviour problems were minimal. More recently I have seen developments along these lines which have moved me even more deeply. Balby Street School in Denaby Main near Mexborough was built in 1908 and has had little added to it since those days. The community it serves is one of the original educational priority areas, and up to a few years ago, when much bulldozing and rebuilding occurred, its back-to-back housing was some of the worst I have seen. At the time when I got to know the school there had been no children of professional parents in it for seven years.

As a mere administrator, I find it difficult to explain even to myself, let alone to others, what it is about this school which has moved me so deeply. The product of the school, its pupils, behave as well as any I have known, and its by-products, its paintings and its writing, are often moving in the extreme. They are an obvious outlet for the pupils' energies and are a source of success which will generate further effort. They build and fortify each child.

As I see it, and again I must emphasize my lack of expertise in these matters, there are three main aspects of a child's expressive work. There is his power of perception and observation, his technical skill, and the depth and intensity of the feeling for what he has seen and experienced. My views on these points are that the teacher's first job is to develop the child's powers of perception and observation by all the means at his disposal. He will, for instance, take children on visits to places of interest and will bring things of beauty and interest into the school, and so do all in his power to stimulate their pleasurable interest in what they observe. He will then encourage his children to express their pleasure and interest in a medium of their choice, and in these and other ways he will do all in his power to stimulate the child's sensitive enjoyment and understanding, and develop him as a person.

The dangers of this kind of work are that after a contrived class experience, the insensitive teacher will force some form of expressive work on his pupils, in a way which may kill the child's zest. Yet another danger is that the teacher in whom the spirit is weak, but who has mastered certain techniques, will impose those techniques on a child in a way which again will deaden the child's spirit by reducing the growth of his initiative, his sensitivity and his inventiveness.

When, however, the expert teacher, as distinct from the technician, can build these qualities of sensitivity and encourage the child to express his own ideas, the spiritual and aesthetic power in the result can be such that an artist would envy. But there are qualities which the teacher must possess before he can do this. He must himself be keenly observant and sensitive to the colour, shape and general beauty of whatever it is that the child is trying to create. He must be able to question and criticize in ways which stimulate and encourage and do not depress. He must have concern and a sincere expectation based on a deep knowledge of the child and his problems and powers. He must be able to share the child's interest and excitement in a way which will draw response from the child.

He must above all be aware that with children of a certain age, and at a certain stage of development, it is possible to deaden the spirit by the ill-timed and ill-understood emphasis on teaching technique.

Unfortunately this kind of expressive work, which can do so much to stimulate the growth of a child as a person, is not susceptible to the kind of measurement by marks and grading which is still the basis of our education service, so that what it can do for a child is to a great extent undervalued. This is a point which will stand further investigation.

2

Loaves and Hyacinths

We live in a world which is growing ever more dangerously materialistic and the education we provide, instead of moderating this materialism, tends to increase it. We are caring more and more for the mind rather than the spirit which we have hitherto so often neglected in our public system.

I remember many years ago going to the house of my aunt, who taught languages to teenage girls including a future prime minister. The following lines hung on her sitting room wall:

> If thou of fortune be bereft
> And of thine earthly store hath left
> Two loaves, sell one, and with the dole
> Buy hyacinths to feed the soul.

Now as I see it, the education which we dispense falls into three fairly clear categories. In the first place, there are the loaves, that is to say the facts that the child has to learn: two and two make four, the Spanish Armada was defeated in 1588, a wild rose has five petals and so on. The characteristics of this kind of learning is that the child gets it right or wrong, and we can measure his accuracy.

Then there is a category where the loaves and hyacinths are mixed. A child learns the 'Ode to Autumn' or he dances a Highland Fling. He can get the words of the Ode right or wrong, and he can get the steps right or wrong, and this is a matter of loaves; but how expressively he recites or how elegantly he dances, the zest, the eagerness and artistry which he brings to these activities is a matter of hyacinths.

But in any good school there will be occasions when a child, probably after a worthwhile and moving occasion, says what he has to say in a way in which he delights, and he can say it in writing, speech, paint, clay, movement, or any other medium of communication which is appropriate, and when this happens the hyacinths stand alone.

In the jargon we tend to diminish the significance of the distinction by referring to the cognitive and the affective, but it is in fact a distinction which goes right through the education process. Putting the loaves first we have for example: the technique of an artistic skill, and the sensitivity, creative power and enjoyment of beauty engendered by its effective use; we have the ability to read and the enjoyment of reading what is worth reading; the facts of history and the visions of good and evil which they reveal; the law of the Old Testament and the love of the New, and so on. The list could be vastly extended.

The loaves are mainly concerned with facts and their manipulation, and they draw on the intellect. The hyacinths are concerned with a child's loves and hates, fears, enthusiasms and antipathies, with his courage, his compassion and his confidence: in short, with a whole range of qualities which determine not what he knows but the sort of person he is and the way he is likely to act.

There is no doubt that the main tradition of education is concerned with the loaves, with the facts, with the intellect, with what can be measured, marked and corrected. There is also no doubt about the fact that it is in the main the 'hyacinths' of life which determine what we do and the way we do it. It is one thing to know how to make an atomic bomb, it is another to decide who is to be killed by its use. Immensely important as the intellect is, it was not mainly intelligence which made Hitler or Jesus Christ the men they were any more than it was mainly intelligence which determined the beauty of the cathedrals at Chartres or Florence or Salisbury.

Why then have we over the years been far more concerned with the loaves than with the hyacinths when educating our children? The answer to this surely is that teaching the facts and the skills which are measurable, in short, dealing with the loaves, has always been the more easily prescribed aspect of education. In the service, on which so much public money is spent, we have gone to extraordinary lengths to make what we do measurable in order that we can make those who do it accountable for what they do.

We have always been and still are prepared to sacrifice the spirit of what we teach in order to achieve this measurability. Indeed the whole vast examination industry on which our education service rests faces an insoluble dilemma; either it puts only those questions to which the answers are right or wrong, thus minimizing judgement, taste, discrimination, wisdom and other great qualities of the human mind and spirit throughout the examination process, or it includes questions designed to test these very qualities and in doing so depends on the subjective assessment of individual examiners, no two of which may award the same subjective marks to the same piece of work. Infinite time and money and intellectual ingenuity are spent trying to solve this essentially insoluble problem.

There is no doubt about the damaging effect of this problem on what is taught and how it is taught. It makes us over-emphasize what is measurable and under-emphasize what cannot be measured. It sacrifices the development of the human spirit to that of the intellect and it makes us distort much of what we teach in an effort to make measurable those aspects of learning, of growth and development which should not be measured.

The examples of what can happen are countless. Those of the past seem to us ludicrous, those of our own day which can be found in many of our current examination papers may well seem ludicrous to those who follow us. It may be worthwhile to look at one or two examples of the kind of thing that can

occur, and at what a few great men of the past have said about
it. When my grandfather began teaching he had to work to a
national code in which everything that he had to do was set out
precisely and was officially tested by HMI. The way of improving a child's English in those days was to parse, so that
when my grandfather was ten he parsed 'Truth lies at the
bottom of a well', which takes up three vertical inches of a
page. When he was twelve, he parsed 'I doubt if he who lolls
his head where idleness and plenty meet enjoys his pillow or
his bread as those who earn the meals they eat', and this took
up nine vertical inches. At fifteen, he parsed the following
sentence, 'He does not scorn it who imprisoned long in some
unwholesome dungeon, and a prey to sallow sickness escapes
at last to liberty and light which the vapours dank and clammy
of his dark abode have bred. His cheek recovers soon its
healthful hue, his eye illumines its extinguished fire, he walks,
he leaps, he runs, is winged with joy and riots in the sweets of
every breeze.' This takes up some fifteen inches, and by my
reckoning, from the age of ten to fifteen my grandfather
completed at least one hundred yards of parsing. To the question 'why?' the answer must be that it was believed that his
English generally would be thereby improved, but a main
point was that the work done could be marked right or wrong.

From a textbook of the time we can learn the examinable
facts about interjections;

Master: How many sorts of interjections are there?
Student: They may all be comprehended in these two sorts, viz.
          solitary or passive, social or active.
Master: Which are the solitary interjections?
Student: These: O! Oh! alas! hey!|hey dey! hark! fie! O fie! O brave!
          O strange! Good sir! Sirrah! tush! pish! wo!
Master: Which are the social interjections?
Student: They denote crying out in a softer manner and seem to
          express love, as 'ho brave boys! soho!', and sometimes
          command as 'here you women!' and sometimes neither, as
          Ha Ha! hush! silence! behold! prithee!

Later on equally precise instructions were given to the Inspectors about the teaching of drawing to infants.

I am to inform you that drawing may be taught to boys in the infant schools on the lines of the Froebel system. Slates ruled with crossed lines marking squares ¼ inch in size should be used and on them children should be made to draw perpendicular, horizontal and diagonal lines. Interest may be given to the exercise by creating figures or patterns out of the combinations developed in this practice, but the main object of the teaching should be the training of the hand to execute with nicety and precision, and the eye to discern degrees of variation in the straight lines from the perpendicular or horizontal, and to compare and judge the relative lengths of the lines and the angles made by their junction.

Arithmetic in my grandfather's day, which of course was either right or wrong, was accompanied by the learning of the arithmetical rule. For example, the rule for long subtraction was

Subtract as in integers only when any of the lower denominations are greater than the upper, borrow as many of that as make one of the next superior, adding it to the upper, from which take the lesser; set down the difference and carry to the next lower denomination for what you have borrowed.

In my youth I had to succumb to the measurable, and I recently came across this kind of work based on Cowper's 'The Task'.

> The cattle mourn in corners where the fence
> Screens them and seem half-petrified to sleep
> In unrecumbent sadness. There they await
> Their wonted fodder, not like hungering man
> Fretful if unsupplied, but silent meek
> And patient of the slow paced swains delay.

Of this we had to learn that 'where the fence screens them' is an example of an adjective sentence introduced by an adverb. Here 'where' equals 'in which'. 'Half-petrified' is an adjective qualifying 'they' (understood) and forming the enlargement of the subject. 'To sleep' is a gerundial infinitive, adjectival in force, qualifying 'they' predicatively and forming the complement of the copulative verb 'seem'. The epithet 'unrecumbent' is transferred from the cattle themselves to the sadness which is associated with them, hence this is an example of Hypallage.

Most of these rules and quotations reveal the exhausting lengths we have gone to in the past to make sure that what was taught was examinable in ways which would enable the teachers to grade their pupils and would make the teachers themselves accountable for what they taught. They either had to confine themselves to the loaves, or make bread of their hyacinths.

When I first came across these examples of past folly, I felt relieved that today we could not do anything as pedagogically stupid as our forebears had done, but there are active moves now current which could make our teachers accountable by assessing the performance of their pupils in such a way that when we have done our assessing, the schools and their teachers will be judged by this performance, be their pupils clever or dull, black or white, privileged or disadvantaged, articulate or incoherent.

We already have evidence in the USA of the sort of thing that can happen and which in my view equals in absurdity anything which our ancestors produced. For instance a year or two ago I came across the following examples of test questions used in the Educational Assessment Program in the State of Michigan.

(1) By the end of the pre-kindergarten experience 90 per cent of all children will demonstrate their recognition of at least three of the five basic emotions: fear, anger, sadness, joy and love in self and others as measured by a future Michigan Educational Assessment Program (MEAP) battery of tests.

(2) By the end of the pre-kindergarten experience 90 per cent of all

children will demonstrate increased understanding of the concept of sexuality.

(3) By the end of the third grade children will create vocal or instrumental accompaniments to songs using combinations of melodic, harmonic or rhythmic patterns as measured by a minimum criteria or an Objective Reference Test or ORT. Example: While the class sings the chorus of 'Oh Susanna', the child plays the tambourine any way he chooses.

(4) By the end of the third grade students will voluntarily choose linear media to interpret personal feelings as measured by a minimum criteria or an ORT.

(5) In the field of physical education the pre-kindergarten children will have 'to express' the mood of music through body movements, walk 10 feet on a straight three-inch taped line (if unsuccessful on the first attempt the children will be expected to be successful on one of the following two trials), to hop five consecutive times using one foot, throw a bean bag into a bushel bag four feet away and tilted at an angle of 45°, and all these achievements will be tested by a teacher-produced/selected instrument or an MEAP test.

This then is the kind of measurability and accountability which the Western world can produce in the 1970s. It is with a vengeance turning hyacinths into loaves. In the past our forebears did this kind of thing in the ignorance of what great men thought of their folly. We do it despite what great men have said.

Dickens in *Hard Times* had no doubt about it. Seeing children sitting in tiered rows in the classrooms of his day, he wrote:

The inclined plane of little vessels arranged in order, ready to have imperial gallons of facts poured into them until they were full to the brim . . . Thomas Gradgrind sir, with a rule and a pair of scales, and the multiplication tables always in his pocket, sir, ready to weigh and measure any parcel of human nature and tell you exactly what it comes to . . . The McChoakumchild School was all fact, the school of design was all fact, the relations between master and man were all fact, and everything was fact between the lying-in hospital and the cemetery, and what you couldn't state in figures or show to be purchasable in the cheapest market and saleable in the dearest was not, and never should be, world without end amen.

Darwin in his *Autobiography* (1887) was more serious:

I have formerly said that pictures gave me considerable and music great delight. But now for many years I cannot endure to read a line of poetry and I have lost my taste for pictures and music. My mind seems to have become a kind of machine for grinding general laws out of large collections of facts. But why this should have caused an atrophy of that part of the brain alone on which the higher tastes depend, I cannot conceive. The loss of these tastes is a loss of happiness and may possibly be injurious to the intellect and more probably to the moral character, by enfeebling the emotional part of our nature.

For Darwin the loaves of immeasurable facts were damaging the hyacinths of art, music, poetry and possibly moral character.

A scientist of similar stature nearer to our time, Einstein, made the same point in *The World as I See It* of 1935:

One had to cram all this stuff into one's mind whether one liked it or not; this coercion had such a deterring effect that after I had gained the final examinations, I found the consideration of any scientific problems distasteful to me for a whole year. It is in fact nothing short of a miracle that the modern methods of instruction have not entirely stamped out the holy curiosity of enquiry, for this delicate little plant aside from stimulation stands mainly in need of freedom without which it goes to wreck and ruin without fail. It is a very grave mistake to think that the enjoyment of seeing can be promoted by coercion and a sense of duty.

For Einstein the loaves of examinable scientific problems, created by coercion and a sense of duty, failed, but only by a miracle, to kill the hyacinths of holy curiosity and the enjoyment of seeing.

Much more recently we have had the recantation by Derek Morell, who founded the Schools Council. I knew him well and I have no doubt that when he took this step he was convinced that it was possible to set out what should be taught and how it should be taught. After a period of service as the senior civil servant in another government department, he produced his recantation in a press article.

When I was at the Schools Council I should have found it difficult to perceive, as I now do, that the curriculum, if it exists at all, is a structure erected on a basis of personal relationships, I should have found it difficult to assert as again I do, that in the curriculum, we are concerned with human beings, whose feelings and aspirations are far more real and immediately important to him than the cognitive development which is the educator's stock in trade.

These are the views of distinguished thinkers who saw the dangers and the folly of sacrificing the hyacinths to the loaves.

The question which at once arises from these views is to what extent do our schools concentrate on the measurable, and neglect more important aspects of the education process which are not susceptible to measurement? It is important in a child's speech and writing that he should be able to record his experiences, but he should also be able to express his feelings. Does the physical education in a school appeal only to the physically gifted or can it also be enjoyed by the clumsy who most need it? Do dance or drama in the school tap the senses and feelings of the pupil, or does he just imitate or perform the techniques in which he is drilled? Is the art of the school something which takes place only in the drawing or painting class, or is the school itself made beautiful with displays of attractive objects and materials contrived by pupils and teachers in such a way that their work will be cherished by all? Is the history or geography of the school learned from textbooks, or is there also knowledge which comes from visits which stimulate and go deeper than textbook information is likely to do? Are there outdoor pursuits, athletics, games, swimming, hiking, canoeing and other activities which will deepen in the best possible ways the relationships which exist between pupils and staff? If these possibilities do exist, then the oil of enjoyment is likely to make the machinery of learning run more sweetly.

Unfortunately there are schools which draw little distinction between information and knowledge. The facts of information are imparted in ways which can be memorized, reproduced and written up at the appropriate examination, but they may lack the interest, excitement and expression which turn them into knowledge.

From my personal experience I would say that some 90 per cent of adults who have followed a course of school and college education have disliked a subject or a teacher, and of these only some 5 per cent have pursued that subject later in life to a more advanced stage. Yet some 75 per cent of any educated groups are likely to have pursued a subject that they enjoyed and this 75 per cent continue with it later in life and will almost certainly know how to transform information into knowledge. They will not only learn the recipe but bake the cake.

Whether they are able thus to move from the loaves to the hyacinths will depend on the convictions of their school and on the educational beliefs of the regime under which it works. If measurement and accountability and blind obedience to the 'basics' are all that matter, many will not get beyond the loaves. But if the things of the spirit, the qualities of personality and the realization of self are seen as the true aims of education, then in the right school many will gather the hyacinths.

3

Some Primary-School Matters

I was recently talking with Miss Canning, an experienced head of an infant and nursery school on a Coal Board estate in South Yorkshire. She is a distinguished teacher who has been much sought after for her advice in this country and in the USA, and she told me what she thought ought to happen in the conditions which will result from the fall in the birthrate. This event, she said, would mean that there would be classrooms to spare and in the poorest of social areas we should use these for the under-threes in order to help those children who had only one parent and those whose mothers had to work such long hours that they were not at home when their children returned from afternoon school. For these and other unfortunate children she would provide an extension of the school day until 6 p.m. She would even go to the extent of providing breakfasts and teas for children in the direst need. She was emphatic in her view that our aim with these children should be the prevention of future trouble rather than equipping the schools to deal with crises as they arose and to this end she would employ a teacher social-worker on the staff of each poorly situated school and this teacher social-worker would bring school and home together well before children reached nursery-school age. Experience has taught her that even amongst the most caring of young mothers there are many who have no idea how to use the simplest speech and play techniques in the home in order to start a child off on the first rung of the educational ladder.

In infant schools in such areas she would convert a redundant classroom into a room for parents. She does not ask for lavish expenditure but she would hope that the room would be comfortable and warm with the simplest of catering facilities. It would be a room where mothers could meet and talk over child-raising experiences amongst themselves or with the staff. There are no doubt schools all over the country where this right kind of development is happening. But there are likely to be many where national and local parsimony are holding 'good' schools back. And by good schools I mean schools which fit this description which came into my hands some time ago.

A good school is a school that has an atmosphere of orderliness, involvement and courtesy, with children moving freely but purposefully in the course of their work.

Voices will be calm but punctuated with moments of excitement. Anger will be minimal, and there will be constant sharing and mutual help. The things around the children will be in keeping with education: books, materials, apparatus, quiet areas, working spaces, play areas, but there will also be things that children find lovely at their visual level, things which will add interest and stimulus to their surroundings, and make their place of work a joy to be in. In the course of their work, the children will visit places of interest outside their school to enrich their experience, and of course there will be full opportunities for conversation about the visits when they return.

There will be an emphasis on play which will create fun and boisterous joy at being out of doors. Physical skill will as far as possible be made available to all and not ruined by excessive competition.

For all, school will be a haven from fear, and because of this, honesty will prevail. It will be a place to be shared with others, a place where it is permissible to make a mess when using materials even if it has to be cleared up afterwards. Thought, reason and logic will be pursued in the desire to discover, a desire which will be shared by the teachers who have a similar liveliness of curiosity. Standards of excellence will be pursued by all.

I have been privileged to know many schools which this description would fit, but at the opposite extreme of the range of school excellence we find this statement given to me by Lord Michael Young and written by him at his most pungent:

The school looked like a mistake. It was in a short red-brick street just behind the defunct cinema which I remember well enough from long ago. It was quite indistinguishable from the red-brick warehouses and factories which surrounded it and it intermingled with them. Neither the factories nor the different sections of the school had any sign to indicate their identity. A derelict warehouse belonging to the school straddled the playground. Mrs S, the headmistress, said the manager was arranging for the building to be made into a canteen. 'The manager' was mentioned several times, and Mrs S seemed somewhat frightened of him.

When we arrived three white-coated ladies were doing something to the remains of lunch in the corridor. But even their efforts with the Irish stew did not squash the pervasive smell of urine. Every time Mrs S's door opened in came another waft. I asked Mrs S about punishments, and she said, 'Oh yes, we have the strap.' 'When did you last use it?' 'Let me see now, you mean officially?' and this raised reverberating visions of countless 'unofficial' strappings. She paused and we thought she was going to say eighteen months ago, or perhaps ten years, as an 'official' strapping was presumably an occasion perhaps in front of the manager. But no, she brightened up and said that the last official strapping was the day before yesterday. 'What was it for?' 'For spitting.' 'Was he warned beforehand?' Mrs S's face got a little red and she incanted, 'Filthy, filthy, filthy, filthy,' in much the same way as she probably did when she laid into the five or six-year-old with her strap. Miss C said that perhaps he was only doing what he did at home. There was silence. Mrs S was probably doing what she did at home; she had six children of her own.

The classrooms were dirty boxes with barely a cupboard in them, decorated with Grand Guignol pictures of Snow White and her Seven Dwarfs. The best teacher had lined her five-year-olds in tables 1 to 9 according to the reading ability of the children. 'These ones there', she said loudly, 'are almost hopeless.' The worst teacher was difficult to credit. Her vacant-faced children were lined up with perfect precision behind their little tables. There was nothing else in the classroom that I could see except a few stray bits of tracing paper, or lavatory paper on which a few children had made desultory marks with wax crayons. A reformatory I went to in Russia for prostitutes who had to work their way back into the world by gargantuan labours on sewing machines was a place of joy compared with this classroom.

I asked the teacher what improvements she would most like to make. She said, 'I'd like to put them in irons.' She meant, as I eventually saw, the desks, though at first I thought she meant the children. But what she wanted was heavy iron desks which these toddlers would not be able to push to the front of the classroom, and in this way the iron ranks would never be broken. I asked whether the children ever moved from their tables during the day, and she answered 'Of course not'.

Asked what she most needed in her school, Mrs S replied, 'A better light in my room.' When the lorries parked up against her window no light came in.

I asked whether there were close relations with the parents and was told yes, of course. She said, 'Why, when a little boy lost his glass eye the other day, one of the teachers went home with him to see it fixed in again.'

The best teacher was a lively girl at the piano. She was not trained but was doing time with a group of eight-year-olds too slow to go into the upper class. The teacher said, 'They'll never learn anything, they can't even learn to sing.' Which was true. The little boy standing on a form in this dirty loft had a great floppy jacket with holes in it, reaching down to his knees, not even cut down from some older brother and perhaps even some small father. The mothers at the entrance were mainly thin and two of them were dressed in felt overcoats. At a house down the road a small boy was crying on the doorstep. I spoke to him. He said his mother had locked him out.

The sad fact of life is that there will always be good schools and bad schools, and the task of any unit of education administration is to narrow the gap between them. Our hope of course is that the newer ways which I saw in those schools which made me change my view will help us to narrow the gap. But we have to bear in mind that at their worst the new ways are almost as bad as anything rigid formal teaching can offer.

We have now produced new kinds of schools to accommodate the 'finding-out' and 'learning-by-doing' techniques, and one of the most remarkable features of this development is that architectural devices have been used to enforce this new fashion for informal teaching. Some new open-plan schools that I have seen in various parts of the world are in my view ludicrous desert spaces where harassed teachers make the best of lamentable conditions. The very sight of these new schools leads one to believe that the cheapness of their box-like accommodation has played its part in forming their shape and content.

One of the most gifted school Advisers I have known, Miss Rae Milne, who worked in the West Riding, insisted that small children need a large classroom where they and their teachers can warmly and securely work together as a group, but nevertheless have some additional space which can be used for shared activities. For somewhat older children in the primary stage it would be better, she said, to have smaller classrooms but a much larger shared area which the children would use for the beginnings of maths and the sciences. In both types of space she asked for alcoves and recesses for quiet individual work. For the secondary stage, she recommended the normal classrooms and separate specialist rooms. In the West Riding we built such schools and the advice we acted upon seems to have been sound as the heads who now work in schools built on this plan commend it. One gifted head, Miss Duckett, who works in such a school made these points:

In the good open-plan school teachers are seen to work and to enjoy their work together, and this sets the right kind of example and atmosphere. Older children have more opportunity to help the younger ones, and this can be exploited by the staff in ways which produce a caring community. Children inevitably have to be trusted to move about an open-plan school on their own volition, and, well handled, this leads to better teacher-pupil relationships. Teachers see each other at work much more closely than in the traditional school, and this can lead to a decrease in the poorer ways of teaching and an increase in the more effective methods, and in general enthusiasm. Furthermore, because of the openness of the building, each member of staff knows far more of what the others are doing and can learn more easily from them.

Miss Duckett admitted that there are problems which can more readily develop in an open-plan school unless they are dealt with as soon as they occur. She mentioned the problem of noise, the difficulties of the traditional classroom teacher who can no longer shut herself off from the rest of the school, the embarrassment of the probationer who fears lest he should parade his weaknesses before his colleagues, the particular ease for creating what Charlotte Brontë would have called a 'swineish tumult', which may be exploited by a single grossly disruptive child. There are also the additional difficulties of record keeping, and of course the 'work dodger' has a greater opportunity to dodge his work. But the head and her staff were convinced that the open-plan school made it far more necessary for them to concern themselves with each child as a growing individual, than as a recipient of a stated amount of factual information, and this, she believed, was a good thing.

Time alone will tell whether the newer ways of teaching will survive long enough to make a permanent change in school building, or whether both methods and buildings will tend to revert to what they were in the middle of the century.

As things are at the present time, I have no doubt that the best of our primary schools are those which use most effectively the methods commended by the Plowden Committee. They are the best because in my experience they produce results in the three Rs which are at least as good as those which come from the best formal teaching that I have ever met with, and they are way ahead in their ability to develop the child's general behaviour and stimulate his spiritual as well as his mental growth.

Unfortunately, though perhaps inevitably, fashion has intervened and we now have teachers and others who talk in clichés and with minimal understanding of 'activity methods, the play way, the integrated day and learning from experience' and yet they fail to realize that all these modern methods are doing is following the advice given by John Locke a few hundred years ago: 'That everyone's genius should be carried as far as it can be.' The result of these methods becoming fashionable is that where they are badly applied bad teaching is the result. This bad teaching then becomes news and inevitably similar schools all over the country, whether good or bad, are splashed with some of the tar from the same brush.

It is of course vastly important that all teachers should consider teaching methods with thoughtful concern. In order to give prominence to method, what I have done is to ask three distinguished teachers how they would teach their subject in such a way that it would be thoroughly disliked. I have done this not as a trick, but to provoke thought. If a teacher reads about sound methods he is apt to say to himself, 'That is what I do.' If however he reads of what purport to be bad methods, and finds in them elements of what he does, he will be likely to think much more deeply.

I asked Mr Harry Wilcock, the head of a junior school, and one of the best teachers of mathematics to young children that I have known, how he would handle his subject without the lubrication of enjoyment, so that as many children as possible would grow to hate it. His recipe was fairly simple.

First of all, arrange the room so that the children cannot speak with one another and keep your place in front of the class to see that they do not attempt to do so. Make sure you consistently criticize every mistake you find, so that the tension of alertness is built up in the classroom. Do not fall into the temptation of letting the severity of your rebukes be moderated by previous good work; be steadfast in making the child realize there is no excuse for error. Make the child utterly reliant on the step-by-step processes you have drilled into him and make sure that he works so many examples, that he can do no other than memorize these processes. The content and level of difficulty of the work done should be determined by what the mathematics books say, and what the scheme of work approved by the headmaster has set out. Don't be led astray by peculiarities of individual children. Let the brightest in the class establish the standards and bring the others on by shaming them in competition and comparisons. To this end, contrive a reward system which will commend the bright, and draw effort from the dull. Do a good deal of quick-time oral work in order to ensure that memory remains more important than deliberation, and to this same end, make the problems as hypothetical and unlikely as possible. Mark vigorously and rigorously and emphasize what is wrong or incorrect. Do not spare the child who deviates from the methods you have prescribed, even if he gets the right answers. In the reports which should be sent to parents twice yearly, do not mince your words when condemning the dull and the lazy and those who lack interest and show little effort.

With concern for the development of the child's sensitivity in mind, I asked a former colleague of mine, Mr W. J. Morrell, a distinguished teacher of English and later a Chief County Adviser, how we would teach it so that it was thoroughly disliked. This is the kind of recipe he gave me:

The subject must be disciplined like mathematics or science. Its main elements, reading, composition, grammar and literature, should be dealt with separately as far as possible, so that each gets its needed emphasis. The children should begin their writing with the simple sentence through to the complex sentence, the paragraph and finally the full composition, which should always be written on a subject chosen by the teacher, and prepared by him with words written on the blackboard. This will assist the ease of marking. If the composition is badly written it should be rewritten and space should always be left for corrections to be written out several times according to the gravity of the error.

Work books which will enable a child to pass normal tests should be regularly used. Some of these blank-filling exercises in textbooks for the young can be very useful, for instance, 'Night is to Day as Moon is to. . .' will help to build up vocabulary. Others such as 'Add "ing" to smile, enjoy and go' will help the child's spelling. There are others aimed at general knowledge such as 'What do we call a mermaid's father?' and yet others again aimed at spelling such as 'Don't shout when in doubt.' Punctuation exercises, comprehension exercises and spelling lists should be constantly used and it is not necessary for the last of these to be associated with what is familiar to the child.

Children should be required to learn pieces of poetry, to recite them, to examine their style, to paraphase their meaning, and to seek out any geographical or historical knowledge they might contain, but recordings of poetry should be avoided as these will inhibit line-by-line examination by the pupils.

As for reading, too much choice can be distracting and it is advisable to use collections of extracts which can be readily adapted to exercises in analysis, comprehension and grammar. Personal collections of books from a children's bookshop should be treated with caution as children should not be allowed to stray too far from the track laid down by the teacher. The school's reading books should of course not be taken home, and all should be covered with thick brown paper.

For advice on how not to teach art to the young, I sought the help of Mrs Ruth Mock, formerly Miss Scrivener, who for some years served as an Adviser in Art in the West Riding. She still teaches and apparently gets incensed by the jargon which prevails in much of the teacher training of our day. She has written her piece on what not to do in the teaching of art as a parody which uses the terms she so deplores.

In our first and middle schools, art has become a module of free expression, free activity and free discipline. A minimal spatial structure is of course necessary, for in this way environmental informality is animated. One or two areas should be liberally furnished with large sheets of paper and card, big brushes, paint, crayons, glue, string, wire, wool, scissors and boxes of scraps.

All paint should be ready mixed so that without any frustration or premeditation each child will be motivated to express in colour, his patterns of sensory perception.

Many ready mixed paints with novel characteristics are available today, and the colours most easily obtained from any source of supply are orange, purple, turquoise, bright green, pink and brown. These are all popular with children so there is no need for others.

At the end of the day, which of course will have been fully integrated, the concept of informality in the classroom situation should not be disrupted by tidying up anything that can be stacked in corners or in cupboards.

Each child must, without the inhibition of imposed behavioural patterns, be motivated to exercise his impulsive creative activity, moving freely in time and space, thus framing with originality his consequential development both cognitive and perceptual.

In the area of perceptual experience there must be no formal structure, and the teacher should never intervene in the child's meaningful processes of sensory experimentation.

The only valid teacher–child dialogue should be in unreserved praise for every manifestation of notional creativity, as the child's personally orientated assurance is all important.

However, with older children in the middle school, the teacher may find that he needs to extend his pupils' abilities in representational illustration to help in the promotion of environmental studies. For this purpose he can provide them with examples of his own work to copy, or add deft touches to what they have tried to produce.

So much for the jargon of art teaching. It is some years since I myself was sufficiently moved against this kind of thing to write my own method for teaching children to walk. It worked out something like this. We need:

(1) A systematic assessment of each child's interests, needs and abilities in walking.
(2) Long range and short range goals in walking for each child based on the interrelationships of his interests, abilities and needs.
(3) The use of alternative methods which would enable each child to reach his short-term objectives, and move towards the achievements of his long-term goals.
(4) Continuous revision of walking goals as the new learning expands the child's potential.
(5) Organizational structure within and without the classroom, which is most likely to facilitate learning to walk.
(6) Adequate support systems to facilitate learning to walk, including consultant services, in-service training, educational and material resources.
(7) A service which effectively measures each individual's mastery of walking and which enables the teacher and the learner to modify and adapt the programme as needed.

No doubt after a time, under such a programme, children would learn to walk, but only the adept would enjoy it.

There is one more point arising from the way we conduct our schools which ought to be mentioned. We are, I believe, the last country of the Western world to beat children with a cane made for the purpose, in order to urge or correct them. On the whole, the nation still believes that when the cane is used rigorously, discipline and behaviour tend to be good, and where the 'rod' is spared, they tend to be bad; moreover the generous use of the cane not only reduces delinquency in school, but tends to avert it in later life.

I once conducted an enquiry into the alleged effectiveness of caning. I approached the Divisional Education Officers of the West Riding LEA, that is to say, the people who knew the schools most intimately, and asked them to tell me which, in their view, were the three best-behaved schools in their areas, and which the three worst. When the lists came in, I handed them to the County Council Inspectors and asked them, without explaining why, to list the schools which used traditional methods of discipline and those which were less formal. I also asked them to talk to the heads, and consult school punishment books, and to let me know which schools used caning most frequently. What emerged from this short study was the fact that the light-caning schools had the better discipline and better behaviour.

I am of course aware of the reservations which must be borne in mind when considering the result of this enquiry. The overall numbers were small, the Divisional Officers' judgement on which were good schools was subjective, appearances before the Juvenile Court, as it was in those days, did not always result in convictions, or in proven association with serious offences. But the enquiry set out to examine the question, 'Is not corporal punishment recognized as a means of averting delinquency later in life?' and certain fairly positive statements can be made in connection with this assumption. For instance:

(a) There is no support for the view that the schools which

cane rigorously produce the best behaviour.

(b) No support whatever for the view that the schools in which the cane is most used produce the fewest delinquents.

(c) There is no support for the view that the school environment does not affect the rate of delinquency amongst children of school age.

(d) There is no support for the view that the best behaved schools in the former West Riding drew their pupils from socially favoured areas.

(e) As far as the schools in this enquiry were concerned, it appeared that behaviour was best, and delinquency least, in those schools where corporal punishment was used sparingly.

Current doubts about the value of beating are supported by the views of many distinguished schoolmasters and educationists of the past. Charles Hoole, who taught in Yorkshire, said this in *New Discoveries of the Old Art of Teaching School* of 1660:

How irksome it is, especially to a man of quiet temper, to have so many unwilling provocations unto passion. . . It is needless trouble to use a rod, and as for a ferula, I wish it were utterly banished out of all schools.

John Locke, probably our greatest educationist, was also firm in his views on this subject, expressed in *Some Thoughts Concerning Education* of 1693:

I believe it will be found that, ceteris paribus, those children who have been most chastised, seldom make the best men . . . The usual lazy and short way by Chastisement and the Rod which is the only Instrument of Government that Tutors generally know or even think of, is the most unfit of any to be used in Education. The Child submits and dissembles Obedience whilst the Fear of the Rod hangs over him: but when that is removed and by being out of sight, he can promise himself Importunity he gives the greater scope to his natural Inclination; which by this way is not at all altered, but, on the contrary heightened and increased in him, and after such restraint, breaks out, usually with more violence. Beating then, and all other

Sorts of slavish and corporal punishments are not the Discipline fit to be used in the Education of those we would have wise, good and ingenuous men.

Roger Ascham was equally certain in his views, in *On Education* of 1711:

(a) But this I will say, that even the wisest of your great Beaters do as oft punish Nature as they do correct Faults.
(b) For in very deed, fond schoolmasters by fear do beat into them a hatred of Learning.
(c) Love is better than Fear, Gentleness better than Beating to bring up a child in Learning.

The simple facts of corporal punishment are that when it is applied, it tends to breed resentment and aggression, whereas when the discipline of a school rests on respect for each other by pupils and teachers, both contribute to the well-being of the community.

This is unfortunately a problem which will never completely be solved, as one cannot ensure that at all times there will be the degree of mutual respect which is necessary to breed responsible and effective relationships, and the use of the cane certainly cannot make up for this kind of deficiency. Fortunately there is reason to believe that the use of the cane, even in our primary schools, is nothing like the menace that it used to be. Far more sinister are the dangers of dull, rigid and weary teaching that one finds in a school which cannot see beyond the 'loaves' of learning, and the opposite dangers of the licence, of ill-understood fashion, that one sees in the worst of what we call our 'progressive' schools.

4

The Advent of the Middle School

The general view of the middle school is that it is a device which has enabled local authorities to turn their existing grammar and modern schools into comprehensive schools as cheaply as possible. Instead of dividing children according to their ability, and putting the clever into one building and the less clever into another, we now divide them according to age, and put the older ones into the former grammar schools and the younger ones into the former modern schools. If the break is made at fourteen it is almost an exact fit, but as this only leaves two years for the secondary school to prepare for 'O' levels, the break has to be made at thirteen or even twelve, and costly building adaptations have to be made.

This simple organizational excuse for the middle school, does not however give a fair picture of what actually lay behind the first experiments. In 1959 the Crowther Committee had said:

The common assumption is, that all comprehensive schools must cover the years from 11 to 18. Need they? Where it is possible to divide these years between two schools the total number on the roll of any one school could be reduced by two or three age groups.

The report gave a number of good educational reasons for

doing this, including the fact that in the eleven to eighteen school, 'The presence of quite young boys and girls involves a paternalism in discipline which often spreads upwards to those who do not need it.'

The Newsom Committee, which followed Crowther in 1963, did not make specific recommendations about the age range of middle schools, but, oddly enough, its terms of reference were 'to consider the education between the ages of 13 and 16 of pupils of average and less than average ability'. The Plowden Committee, which reported in 1967, was more positive, and after much thought and careful reasoning, recommended that there should be primary schools for children of five to eight years, and that these should be followed by middle school for pupils of eight to twelve years.

The great debate in those years was whether the primary-school attitudes and techniques should move upwards into the new middle schools, or whether secondary specialization should move downwards. In the years when this was a source of much discussion, primary schools of the informal variety were flourishing. Many of them were very good schools indeed, and they received Plowden approval. In more recent years there has I suspect been a decline in the quality of such schools, and we shall not know for some time which way they are likely to go. It is however interesting to look back at what was hoped for from middle schools, and what were the educational reasons behind their formation.

In 1962, five years before the Plowden Committee reported, I had to face the problem of whether or not the West Riding should adopt a middle school way of turning comprehensive in some of its most densely populated areas, notably Hemsworth. To help my Committee to make up its mind I listed fifteen of the most notably gifted educationists amongst the heads in the service of the Authority: heads of primary schools, secondary schools and colleges of education, and put specific points to them. We asked them what age they would choose for transfer to the secondary school, and ten of them chose thirteen. They pointed out that thirteen was the age of transfer in the private sector of education, and emphasized their conviction that in any secondary school the first and second year are easy to teach and 'playing up' does not start until the third year. They affirmed that much of the energy which youngsters display at about thirteen might be turned to good account if there was a change of school at that time.

It was pointed out that the age of 11 plus had been decided in the main by the simple device of subtracting three from the school leaving age of fourteen at a time when three-year senior schools were established under Hadow reorganization. There was also at that time a most marked demand for the extension of good primary-school techniques. The head of one large grammar school wrote: 'I think I would like to see a middle school develop along lines more nearly resembling those along which the best junior schools are moving, than as a junior version of the present secondary school.' The principal of a college of education said: 'I very much like the idea of transfer at 13. It makes it possible to extend some of the advantages of the enlightened primary school approach.'

The County Council Inspectors had their own point of view:

Generally speaking, children in the age group 9 to 11 would work as they do in the primary school at present. This type of teaching would continue through the 11-13 stage, but it would be natural to expect groupings and settings which would allow specialist teachers to follow their interests. The widest variety of organizations could arise here, but even at the top of the school children should be working in uniform classes for only about half of their time.

From the head of a secondary modern school: 'Up to the age of 13 years an extension of the kind of work so admirably done in the best primary schools would, in my view, be more in keeping with the development of the child.' One grammar school head dealt with the examination problem by the terse statement that one of the great advantages of the break at thirteen would result from the fact that staff, thinking in terms of GCE syllabuses, would not be able to 'get at' children of eleven to twelve years of age.

The question of specialization was raised, and none of those approached favoured the kind of organization which has for so long characterized much secondary-school teaching. What emerged was the idea that the break between primary and secondary school which normally takes place between July and September of any given year should be spread over four years with the amount of specialist working increasing from year to year. But there was a strong demand that from the outset art, the crafts, and drama and music should play a large part in the programme of the school, and teachers should be appointed who could work in these subjects at a fairly advanced level. It followed that these ideas would inevitably affect the school building and that the shared areas, which would increase in size for the older pupils, would contain apparatus and equipment necessary to accommodate the increased time spent on specialist activities.

The first purpose-built middle school that I know of has now been in use for ten years and there are others in the area formed by adaptation. The head of the comprehensive school to which most of these schools send their children told me recently that he would not happily revert to seven to eleven primary schools. He maintains that this type of organization moved the weaker pupils from the infant school to the junior school just at the time when they should be consolidating their ability to read. But there is no doubt that many comprehensive schools do not accept that it is part of their job to continue to teach reading to all normal children even if they are prepared to teach it to a remedial group. The point which still remains has already been mentioned, it is whether in the middle schools enlightened primary ways are to work upwards, or whether the preparation for examinations, so typical of the secondary stage, it is to work downwards and invade the middle-school age range. Obviously there is greater examination pressure on the nine to thirteen school, and there is a danger of a deliberate split in such a school with the nine to eleven group continuing with primary-school methods while those who are twelve to thirteen specialize particularly in such subjects as science and maths. When such divisions do occur, the difficulty is in finding specialist teachers who are satisfied with such a young and narrow age range when they have the ability and the will to tackle some general and more advanced teaching. A further danger lies in the temptation to over-supply the top of the nine to thirteen middle school with sophisticated equipment and apply it to the slowest youngsters for whom it may be unsuitable. There is of course a sex difference between the eight to twelve and nine to thirteen ranges in that many thirteen-year-olds are already young women.

The ultimate judgement on the middle schools will have to be postponed for a few years, until the degree of their success becomes evident. But there is no doubt that the way they eventually go will to a great extent be determined by what happens in the meantime to primary-school teaching.

5

Some Secondary-School Matters

When the Education Service was established in 1870 the schools that were drawn into it were in some ways comprehensive schools. Each tended to serve a defined neighbourhood and though the children were graded according to ability rather than age, the abilities, particularly in village schools, were so diverse that inevitably there was some mixed-ability teaching. Moreover, there was in most schools a mixture of social groups, though of course the most affluent parents sent their children away to schools that would prepare them for 'the great public schools' as they were called, and somewhat less affluent parents used local private schools. The main objectives of such parents was to secure what they thought was good teaching for their offspring and to avoid their coming into contact with children whom they judged to be 'common'.

When the secondary schools were established by the Act of 1902, things changed. New county secondary schools were built and were highly selective. They took their curriculum in the main from the older grammar schools and the Independent 'public' schools. Latin was basic, but in the new schools somewhat more emphasis than was traditional was given to maths and science. As far as 'character' was concerned, this was dependent on the school assembly with its daily dose of religion, on organized games and on the cane. Before external exams took control some of these schools were admirably innovative and civilized places in which to learn.

But there were two innovations which distinguished the new schools from the elementary schools which supplied them. The first was that the new county secondary schools admitted not only fee-paying middle-class children but poor working-class scholars who gained their admission on the result of a gruelling County Minor Scholarship examination which Sir Graham Savage, formerly the country's senior HMI and later the Director of Education for London, described to me in these terms: 'It was a test which on a chosen Saturday lasted from 9 a.m. to 12 noon and from 2 p.m. to 5 p.m. There were tests in Arithmetic and English, including a separate paper in Grammar, and tests in History, Geography and Drawing.' The emphasis was on the selective procedure designed to pick out the clever from the mass and the belief was held that those who won the County Minor Scholarships would be able to move up in the social scale to professional status, while the rest were left to do as they could in the upper years of the elementary schools, a path which at best would lead them to manual labour. This social distinction established by the new scholarship tests gave rise to immediate social tension between the selected and the unselected children. The failures tended to regard those who succeeded as 'swanks'; and they used the most offensive adjectives they knew to revile them. The two groups would fight in the streets and the times of opening and closing of schools were in some areas made to differ in order that the two groups should not meet on their way to and from school, and behave in ways which offended their elders.

Selection has been a bane ever since it was first introduced; it moved from the traditional formal tests of composition, dictation and repetition to the intelligence test, the inventors of which convinced themselves and others of its accuracy. The result was that when the test had to select five children out of 100 for admission to the grammar schools, errors were relatively low, but when one test had to select twenty or twenty-five children out of each 100 and send those so selected to the grammar schools things were very different. The error made, it is true, was only 10 per cent of all who were examined, but this meant that of every 100 children five or six who ought to have stayed in the elementary school were moved into the secondary school and the same number who should have been selected were in fact rejected. In other words, according to subsequent tests some half of those pupils admitted to secondary schools were wrongly placed.

Most examiners and many teachers were fully aware of these forms of fallibility and it was a common occurrence in those days for those who conducted the examination to refer to the high 'Highs' and the low 'Lows', when talking of children who had done in the test what was expected of them. But the disturbing comment was when the adults in charge spoke of the high 'Lows' and the low 'Highs', that is to say those who had done well at school but who came down in the test, and those who were dull at school but who excelled themselves in the test. The tests thus came under suspicion and criticism as it is seldom that a teacher who has taught a bright child over a considerable period of time is prepared to admit that he and not the test is at fault when the clever fail or the dull succeed.

But the major damage which a test can do is to create failures. Many a slow child whom the school ought to build and fortify may be well on the way to achievement when the examination throws him back into despair and brands him as a failure. It is as if we entered a cripple for a sprint and then when he fails, as inevitably he must, we blame him for lack of competence or endeavour.

The problem of selection following the 1944 Act became much more serious. In the period between 1902 and 1944 we had sought to select 'clever' children and pass them on at the age of eleven to our selective schools. But in 1944 we were told by the new law that we had to select children according to their age, ability and aptitude, and this was a task that many of us in administration at that time had difficulty in doing, and it was an occasion when the politicians and officials at the Ministry of Education fell into difficulties of their own making.

In those days, the Ministry believed in the tripartite system of grammar schools, technical schools and modern schools and set out their belief in a publication called *The Nation's Schools*. The belief was supported by an investigating body, the Norwood Committee, which in its report (1943) divided children into three categories: 'those who loved learning, those who wanted to apply it, and those who dealt with concrete things'. So convinced were the Ministry about all this that when after the war they required LEAs to produce their Development Plans, which were to promote educational revival and reconstruction, the Ministry demanded that 10 per cent of all secondary-school places should be 'technical' in their nature.

I was a very inexperienced Education Officer of a very large Authority at this time, and the requirement baffled me as I did not believe it to be possible. So I wrote to some of the most distinguished educational thinkers of the day, Sir Fred Clarke, Sir Godfrey Thomson and Dr Charlotte Flemming, and asked them how to detect technical aptitude in an eleven-year-old child. All three wrote back saying in their several ways that it could not be done, and by this time Sir Cyril Burt had written an article in which he said that 'Any scheme of organization which proposes to classify children at the age of 11 according to qualitative mental types rather than according to general intelligence is in conflict with the known facts of child psychology.'

I then wrote to the Ministry and asked them if they would kindly tell me how to select children according to their aptitude, and after a long delay the conflict of views was resolved in a way not unknown to administrators. One day my telephone rang and the voice of a senior civil servant from London whom I knew well said, 'Look, Clegg, do you really want an answer to this damn silly question of yours?' and I replied, 'Not if you will go easy on that damn silly stipulation then agreed that the correspondence at both ends should be taken from the files. But of course the problem remained and the post-war Development Plan had to be prepared.

The West Riding Committee, which I served at that time, resolved to do all in its power to ensure that wherever possible some form of advanced work should take place in each kind of secondary school, be it grammar, technical or modern, so that 'No child with specific abilities and ambitions should be trapped in a type of school in which those ambitions could not be realized.' As for the future, it was decided 'that the Authority should continue wherever possible, the policy it had already adopted in 1944 at Tadcaster of building community schools to take all types of children in the area, but not sufficiently large to become unwieldy.'

We were then in the mid-forties, and were already disturbed by the threat of size. We believed that about one-fifth of the age group could follow a grammar-school course, but that a one-form-entry grammar school was too small to be viable. On the other hand, if we admitted to every secondary school two grammar school forms of thirty each, and these formed one-fifth of a comprehensive school, that school would eventually approach 2000 which we believed to be too big. Eventually the view taken was that 'this argument is only correct up to a point, for though it is true to say that a single-stream grammar school cannot be adequately staffed, in a large school of 800 to 1000 pupils there should be quite enough well-qualified members of staff to provide for most types of sixth-form work.' And thus the policy of the authority in 1946 was to aim at comprehensive schools of 800 to 1000 pupils and this policy was expressed in a preface to their Development Plans in these terms:

The Committee have given their most earnest attention to the task of realizing the basic conception of the 1944 Act of Secondary Education for all pupils. In defining their policy towards secondary education, they have been unable to accept certain suggestions which have been made or implied in various reports and ministerial circulars. They cannot for instance agree that children at the age of 11 can be classified into recognized mental types and should be allocated to Grammar schools, Technical schools and Modern schools accordingly, or that numbers to go to the various types of secondary schools should be determined by an arbitrary percentage of the age group.

What they eventually decided was that 'the school which admits all children of an area at the age of 11 years, and exposes them to a variety of practical, social and intellectual experiences, offers the greatest possibility of adjusting educational treatment to the needs of the individual child.'

That an Authority such as the West Riding, which was fairly evenly divided between Socialists and Conservatives, was able in the forties to accept a policy which aimed at comprehensive schools, but left the decision very largely for the locality to choose, is a fairly clear indication of how slight the political pressure for or against comprehensive schools was in those days. Indeed, the first half dozen comprehensive schools in the West Riding were in fact established in Conservative or Liberal areas (Tadcaster, Calder Valley, Penistone, Colne Valley, Settle and Elland). At the other political extreme, the coalfield which had always looked with pride on its grammar schools and had seen in them an escape route from a dismal area, looked upon the comprehensive idea with suspicion.

In the West Riding the decision to establish the first multi-lateral school was taken in 1944 by the governors of Tadcaster Grammar School, at that time a solidly Conservative body who quite rightly decided that it would be stupid to build three separate schools, one grammar, one technical and one modern in a town as small as Tadcaster, and what they wanted was one school with several sides to it. Other Conservative areas took a similar decision within a short time and the fact that their decisions had to be taken on purely educational grounds meant that those responsible were still relatively unmoved by political reactions even after the Labour Party had adopted comprehensive schools as one of their major political aims.

But it was one thing to establish one major school in each small township; it was quite another to establish a pattern of such schools in a major city. I have been fortunate to secure the story of what happened in London from Sir Graham Savage who, as I have already said, was until 1940 the Senior Chief Inspector of the Ministry of Education, and who thereafter became the Chief Education Officer of the London County Council.

Savage was deeply disturbed when he realized that his task was no longer to select the few children who, because of their high marks, would be excused the payment of all or part of the school fees, but to examine all children and allocate them to schools of different types, taking into account their aptitudes as well as their age and ability. He knew from experience what a chancy thing selection at eleven years was. As he put it:

Success in the grammar school by fee payers was not noticeably better or worse than that of scholarship holders. One of the heads in my London district kept a very close record on all this, and particularly directed his attention to a comparison of the record of his 'scholars' and that of his fee payers chosen from the runners-up in the selection exam. There was virtually no difference between the groups when later they were measured by the results of the School Certificate examination.

Another issue was the question of the age allowance at 11 plus. The London records revealed that age dominated the 11 plus exam, and that those who were 11 and one-twelfth had a very small proportion of successes compared with those who were 11 and eleven-twelfths, but when the authority tried to compensate by an age allowance, Savage's view was that this tended to make a nonsense of the test.

There was one other problem which apparently worried both London and the West Riding. Savage had realized that 'one mark on the London list would separate hundreds of children into different categories and schools, and one mark moreover, on a test of very dubious validity.' I made the same point when I told my Committee that 'the decision as to whether a child is admitted to a grammar school or not may depend on a margin as small as one-fifth of one per cent in an examination taken on one day in his twelfth year.'

It was this kind of intractable educational point which turned some administrators of over thirty to forty years ago towards the comprehensive pattern of secondary schooling. Their political masters at the time took a different view. Attitudes towards comprehensive schools became political and the politics of those days still persist. In the country as a whole, the politicians of the Left were the first to move. In the fifties they adopted the comprehensive principle in the naive belief that if all children went to the same school, social differences between them would be ironed out. The extreme Right opposed the new left-wing belief out of fear lest there should be something in it. Their fear was that class distinctions might be diminished in ways which they would deplore. One curious fact about the West Riding was that two grammar schools, each several hundred years old, were the first to turn comprehensive and the change was brought about well and wisely by right-wing politicians.

Since those days in the early and mid-forties the greater part of the county has accepted the comprehensive principle and we can expect significant development as these schools become more mature, more practised and more understanding.

What we have to ensure is that these new schools achieve the highest standards which our present parsimonious era will permit and we must not fall into the well-worn educational trap of finding a bad comprehensive school and then blaming the comprehensive pattern for what may be caused by a poor head, a bad background, an ungenerous Authority, a staff which is too young or too old, or any one of a host of causes which have nothing whatsoever to do with the school being comprehensive.

I do not know a comprehensive school which I would describe as a bad school though I am sure that given a day or two I could find one. When in office, I knew from experience in my job of a number of poor grammar, technical and modern schools, but at the time of which I write very few comprehensive schools had been in existence long enough to become bad. More recently I have visited and got to know a number of comprehensive schools and from each I have learned much and gained encouragement.

When I first became an Education Officer my three sons became pupils in the first neighbourhood multilateral school in the county. They did so not because of my belief in the principle but because the local multilateral school served the village in which we lived. What I admired about that school at the time was that weaker pupils who needed the most help were put into the smaller classes and so were given more attention.

In another area a grant from the Carnegie Foundation enabled the Authority to build a school in a tough district around a carefully planned social centre. It became a community school, to the art and craft rooms of which young shift workers returned in their spare time. It provided a pre-school playgroup which was run by senior girls and by mothers who wished to help, it brought together as a measure of support a committee on which were represented local magistrates, social service staff, representatives of the health service, the police, probation officers and others concerned with the welfare of the teenager.

One of the major problems that comprehensive schools have had to face is that of size, as there is little doubt that sheer size can create problems of discipline and control. In the early days of comprehensive growth the larger units used generally to be divided into upper, middle and lower schools. More recently some schools have divided the thirteen to sixteen-year-olds into houses and joined them across the top, as it were, by a sixth form. I know of one such school where there was considerable vandalism in some of the lower rooms of the school building. This was tackled and eventually cured by dividing the school into four houses, each under a Head of House, and each house being responsible for its own curriculum, timetabling, recreation and discipline, and its contact with parents.

The abused rooms were redecorated and refurbished by the pupils and handed over to them and to responsible teachers with obviously beneficial results. This form of organization was welcomed when it was introduced some years ago and the school still firmly believes in its effectiveness.

Yet another school in a deep industrial area won over the energy and resource of its pupils by carefully planned projects in school time which involved caving, canoeing, camping and sailing. They also developed a programme of help for old people in hospital and the young ones in their playgroup. They twice won a national nature conservancy award for a project which restored and beautified a piece of derelict land for the benefit of the community. This same school developed a scheme whereby it visited and was visited by an independent school of national repute. The two schools got to know each other as they took part in joint efforts which were carefully prepared and have led to a valuable union which after a number of years still exists.

It would of course be nonsense to infer from these few projects that their quality and progress were a direct outcome of the comprehensive principle. But there is no doubt that having to care for the slow and the quick in the same intimate environment can give rise to a spirit which urges that not merely the gifted, but all the pupils in a school be treated according to their needs.

Few who have not had the experience realize how intense is the endeavour which has to be exerted if the best is to be done for all pupils whatever their background and ability. I have had the satisfaction of watching over a period of years what has been done in a school which serves one of the most harsh industrial areas that I know of. How the change was brought about has been worthy of study.

The school to which I refer is a school of 1500 pupils. Some 80 per cent of its pupils are born of semi-skilled and unskilled workers. The school began as a modern school; the building consisted of the longest school corridor I have ever seen, with classrooms leading into it. It was the dullest school building of its time that I recall. It was turned into a neighbourhood comprehensive school, but was virtually a bilateral school: a grammar school and a modern school under one roof. Order was maintained by strict authority reinforced by the cane. The children were divided into the bright ones who would take 'O' levels, and the rest who would not. The former were taught by teachers with grammar-school experience and given all that they needed by way of resources. In order to grade the pupils the school divided the subjects of the curriculum into two groups. Each subject in the first group, and these included maths, science, English and a foreign language, carried a maximum of 200 marks. The subjects of the second group included music, the arts and a variety of crafts, and each of these carried only 100 marks. A thick black line on the mark sheet divided these two groups and enabled one teacher to say, 'You know I'm only a below the line teacher.'

When a new head came to the school he was at first impressed by much of what he saw when the school was in session, but the shock came outside during the morning break, and in the lunch hour on the school bus park, as the children made for home. The school doors had to be guarded during the breaks in order that children should not re-enter the building before the permitted time and do damage. Police undertook a daily duty outside the building when, after school, the buses collected the children to take them home. There was much fighting and obscenity. Teachers on duty were spat upon and kicked, and two were even knocked unconscious, and the teachers were told, 'You can't do owt to me now, it's out o' school time.'

The new head soon found out that his traditional grammar-school teachers could not cope with the lower-ability groups, and when they tried to serve up a thinned academic diet, all that happened was that a resentment was built up in the less responsive youngsters; a resentment which often led to frustrations and confrontations. The young and inexperienced teachers were given the slower learners, and their difficulties were such that they seldom stayed in their post for more than two years.

There were more shocks for the new head as he went about the school. It became obvious to him that relations between staff and pupils were strained. Children were expected to obey orders, to fetch and carry and be taught. There was seldom any friendly conversation between the two groups. The head went into one classroom where the teacher said to him in a voice audible throughout the room: 'We shall get some 'O' levels from these five in the front, but that lot at the back haven't a hope.' On another occasion he asked one boy what sort of reading books he liked, and the boy made the revealing reply that he liked them thin, with large print and a lot of pictures. All that the new head saw made him realize that he was diametrically opposed to much of what was going on in the school, and that if he were to survive he would have to encourage the introduction of change. This he did gradually, with the support of the more caring members of his staff, and he was fortunate in having the full backing of a very influential and able Chairman of Governors.

Now on entering the school the children are grouped according to the area in which they live and the friendships they have formed in the primary school. They remain with the group as they go through the school. If however anything happens which makes it beneficial to withdraw a child from the group — if for instance he is grossly disruptive, if he wants to do additional mathematics, or science, if he needs more help with a language — he may be withdrawn for periods for this purpose, but he will still remain as a member of his initial group.

The main difference which I now see in this school is that the children in difficulty and children in the lower-ability range matter. The teacher who leads their group is their mentor and friend, and the school's general concern and recognition is much more fairly distributed than used to be the case. The crafts are important in the school and exhibitions of the pupils' artwork have been held in the local Miners' Welfare Centre.

The headmaster himself teaches twelve periods a week and distributes his teaching between the first year, the third year and the fifth year. He takes the more difficult groups, and he claims that it does the staff good to see him struggling. He also gives every support to the school choir and the folk groups, the school band and the school games. He is available in his room to everyone in the school — children and staff alike, and I have not the slightest doubt that his friendliness and his deep conviction that all children matter is responsible for the quality which is developing in this school.

Provision of a most unusual kind has been made for those who are in real difficulty, or who need special help. The Chairman of the Governors presented the school with some fairly derelict buildings. These are being rehabilitated and decorated by those of the pupils who need the confidence which derives from successful achievement. Moreover, not only do the youngsters study in this new environment under the guidance and direction of a gifted teacher, but parents now play a significant part in maintaining the building and manning its refreshment bar. The mothers for instance collected several hundred pounds to help with the refurbishing of the restored building. In addition to this venture, the school pursues a number of outside activities: canoeing, sailing, camping and the like — and these activities are in fact time-tabled. Travel is made possible by using the three cars which the school owns and in which children learn to drive.

Each youngster has a very large element of choice in his curriculum. There is a range of craft courses, all of which both boys and girls may adopt. These include not only the traditional crafts but such activities as motor vehicle maintenance and a 'school enhancement' course.

A regular bulletin is issued to parents and a list is sent to them each month of the concerts and theatres to which they may choose to go with their children if they so wish. Similarly a list of industrial works to be visited is issued to the pupils each month.

The children are offered a wide range of academic subjects at 'O' level, and the CSE course includes the school's special study on family life and the community. The school offers twenty-four subjects at 'A' level. Children at risk are given special attention by one of the seventy teachers, each of whom has the care of a group of children, with the result that all of the seventy gain some knowledge and experience of careers, slow-learners, curriculum-advice, disruptive youngsters and other vital matters, and this means that any youngsters, boys or girls, can identify their need and look for help in meeting it.

Two other points need to be made about the school. Their examination results are far better than I expected; they are in fact very good indeed. Perhaps more important still is the fact that at a time when juvenile delinquency is on the increase the cases from this school dropped from sixty-one and seventy-six in the year 1971–72 to twenty-six and forty-eight in the year 1976–77.

I have mentioned the school in some detail because I know of the difficulties it has overcome. But the important point which ought to be made is that over the country there must be many schools like this, each of which is struggling to find new ways of helping the current generation of young people to overcome the danger and difficulties which the older genera-tion have thrust upon them, or at least allowed to develop around them. The education service ought to know more about what is possible, and can be shown to be possible, for in that way — and I suspect in that way only — lies the real path of progress.

I suspect that in schools of this kind, because of the way in which the staff are handled, there are more teachers than is usual who could answer the question, 'Why am I teaching what I am teaching in the way I am teaching it to these particular pupils at this time in their lives?'. I sometimes think that many schools do what they do either because the external exam demands it, or because it has always been done. I con-sider myself fortunate to have worked with colleagues who have so often compelled me to ask 'why?' and there are few people if any, to whom I owed more in this respect when Education Officer in the West Riding than I did to the late Diana Jordan. She began as an Assistant Adviser in Physical

Education. From this modest position she produced the detailed principles and plans which resulted in the new teachers' colleges at Wentworth Woodhouse and Bretton Hall, and in 1952 she planned, established and became the Warden of Woolley Hall which was one of the first if not the first residential in-service training centre for teachers in the country. But she did more than this. She used from time to time to send me minutes which threw light on much that we were all trying to do. I came across one of these sent to me in July 1955 under the heading 'The Architecture of Subjects'. She was concerned with why we do what we do and she wrote as follows:

If I had to organize the work of a secondary school I would group my teachers of special subjects so that they realized how their particular subject formed part of the five corner stones of the education we provide, and these would be related to the pillars of my structure which would be the qualities which I believe can and should be developed in children of 11 to 16 years of age.

These would be my subject groups or corner stones:
(1) Religious Education, English, Drama and History.
(2) Geography, the Sciences and Mathematics.
(3) The Crafts, Domestic Subjects and Rural Studies.
(4) Art, Music and the Dance.
(5) Physical Activities, including skills, agilities, games, swimming, camping, hiking and cycling.

The 'pillars' of my structure, the qualities I would aim at, would be related to the groups:
(1) The first group of subjects would promote a vision of greatness, an awareness of a respect for human inheritance, an understanding of human motives and human relationships, verbal communication and expression and a reverence for life itself.
(2) My second group, science and mathematics, would lead to curiosity, to a thirst for knowledge and would foster a sense of wonder and responsibility.
(3) My third group would form the pillar based on creativity and craftsmanship and on the establishment of those standards and values needed in the making of a good home.
(4) My fourth group, art, music and the dance, would cultivate the senses and promote aesthetic values, and the communication of

feelings by non-verbal means of expression.

(5) My fifth would be a pillar made up of physical courage, self-discipline, responsibility and good personal relationships.

Each group would be aware of the limitations of the subjects which formed it and would appreciate fully not only the necessity for co-operation within the group, but with other groups.

All children need recognition, self-esteem and security. These can come from the satisfaction in making things, tools, patterns, pictures, models, fabrics, foods and so on, and this is the way the crafts should develop. They should not be separated for boys and girls or into different subjects, but should be inter-related so that shape, function, colour and texture can be fully enjoyed in whatever form they take.

Words well used can also bring confidence to a child, and teachers should not tolerate 'sort of this' and 'kind of that' but should get their pupils to enjoy searching for the right word or phrase. English must mean all this and the distaste for it brought about by ill-used grammar, spelling and comprehension exercises must be avoided. Above all, books must be loved. Some will gain their self-esteem from the arts, which will enable them to communicate in ways other than words. Dance for instance, which uses the pulses and patterns of the body, will give the child experience of moods and heighten them in ways which revitalize.

As for music, every child should have the opportunity to succeed with his voice or an instrument or both. They should also learn to delight in the sounds of nature, such as bird song, and in the sounds of primitive drums and rhythms.

And there is of course physical education. Just as in recent years art has revealed to us what children can do when freed from the tricks of imposed techniques, so movement education is beginning to show the real wealth of physical skill that lies within all children when they are not subjected to the adult exercises and tricks which are often devised merely as a corrective. What really matters is enjoyment; the enjoyment of skill, adventure, and comradeship, and games should not be merely *the* hockey period or *the* football practice. There should be more games for both large and small areas, for the skilled and the unskilled, and we should cultivate not only gymnastics, track athletics, dancing, swimming, and field events, but drama and of course hiking, light-weight camping, mountaineering and excursions of all kinds. We should bear in mind what Herbert

Read said about movement, 'It is the basic art merging organically into music, drama and all the other arts and crafts. This is what the Greeks realized so clearly, and one could find plenty of support for the idea in modern psychology.'

These are the somewhat idealized hopes of one who spent much of her life looking at fine work in schools and in bringing together those responsible for it in the firm belief that quality and standards can be raised by encouraging discussion and criticism amongst those responsible for them.

The need for discussion grows as our weaknesses increase, and there are many weaknesses. The curriculum is likely to continue to benefit by the work of such bodies as the Schools Council, the Subject Associations and even the external examinations, but there are other facets of the education service which are likely to suffer.

Selection will continue and children who need to be strengthened by success will be damaged by failure. Class distinctions are likely to continue in the schools of the future. We shall still have public, assisted, and maintained schools comparable to Oxbridge, York and Lancaster and Redbrick at the University level.

Juvenile vandalism exists in this country as in the very different countries of Europe and the Americas, and none seems yet to have mastered it. With the development of the computer there is likely to be more time in which petty villainy can flourish, and the techniques of vandalism will spread and become more sophisticated. Beauty in our schools will diminish with lack of funds, and the Councillors who believe that this matters are relatively few.

The assessment of performance flourished at the end of the last century and did vast damage to the education service. Will those who believe in it today manage to harness its usefulness while minimizing the damage which it can do?

Will assisted places in independent schools be increased? Their success will reintroduce the direct-grant principle. I looked into this some years ago and discovered that pupils with an IQ as low as 110 were admitted to our ordinary grammar schools and only 6 per cent of them had an IQ of over 135. In the direct-grant schools serving the same area no child with an IQ of less than 125 was admitted from the West Riding and 50 per cent of all admissions from the Riding had an IQ of 135 plus.

It remains to be seen whether the assisted pupil project will in fact be used by Authorities to bolster up Independent schools. Will the choice of school and the voucher system be used to revive failing schools? If so, how will choice of school be managed? To take an extreme case: if there are two inner city schools — A and B — within a mile of each other and all the parents of the area choose school A for their children, will school B be closed and school A doubled in size? I have seen and was partially responsible for clever children from the maintained grammar school in Morley travelling by bus to the aided grammar school a few miles away in Batley, while the slower children in Batley travelled to fill the places vacated by the bright children from Morley. This scheme was, in my view, one of the most stupid and unreasonably costly in which I have ever had a part.

Will the choice of school apply equally in both town and country areas? If so, how far each day are children in rural areas to be permitted to travel? There will be a continuing problem of migrant children, and it is one which may get worse before we get the better of it.

But the major issue which faces us is what is to be done about our slower learners, particularly as the demand for their labour grows less. Mr George Shield, a headmaster of considerable repute, put the matter to me in these terms:

I am one who believes that the invention of CSE will yet be seen to be an ill-considered move with potentially catastrophic consequences. Despite valiant efforts to develop Mode 3 papers in at least one part of the country, CSE has succeeded in imposing upon a substantial proportion of the population a pattern of studies and a burden of examination requirements which may be demanded by employers but have little real relevance to the needs of the jobs the students are to do. More importantly the pattern is seen by many of the pupils to have little relevance to their own interests. In truth, neither the study courses nor the examination itself has any great relevance to the world of work or the world of leisure despite the fact that it is being used as a random but 'essential' requirement by many employers. Worse still it places into a sadly depressed minority group a clearly recognized set for whom even these limited CSE aims proved to be beyond reach and has thus succeeded in identifying and labelling total failure and inadequacy in a whole stratum of youth.

It is one of the more astonishing facts of recent years that the education service has paid but slight attention to this kind of warning, even though it was given twice with extreme clarity and insistence by no less a body than the Central Advisory Council. The Council, when it was studying the education of children of fifteen to eighteen years under the chairmanship of Sir Geoffrey Crowther, said 'The majority of children in modern schools ought not to be subjected to the external examination and their interest must be protected.' In the summary of the appropriate chapter of the report occurs this statement: 'many, probably more than half, of the pupils of the modern schools would have their education deflected from its proper lines by being prepared for an external examination. It is important that attention to the needs of a minority should not be allowed to lead to the neglect of the interests of these boys and girls who are and will remain by far the largest single group in the modern schools. All our other recommendations are subject to this.'

Newsom, dealing in the main with the lower half of the ability range, spoke strongly and said: 'We are convinced that many of the pupils with whom this report is concerned should not be entered for public examinations and that for all pupils a substantial part of the curriculum should be unexamined.'

It is probably views of this kind that moved Lord Butler, who by his Act of 1944 made our education service complete, to say recently to the press: 'I believe that the death of the 11 plus examination combined with the birth of the comprehensives are the most significant developments of education in the past decade.

It would be possible greatly to extend this list of grave problems which our secondary schools have to face. But there are two possible ways in which relief and progress may be sought. The first is that the aim of our education, particularly when dealing with the slower pupils, is for their teachers to ensure for each pupil, not necessarily the ability to pass an examination, but a sense of real achievement on which personality and ability can be built and nourished. The second major point is that good practice must be more readily identified, and schemes inaugurated whereby teachers facing similar problems may get together in such a way that each learns something of how the others succeed, particularly with the slower learners of whom Edward Thring, headmaster of Uppingham, wrote in these terms in his book *Theory and Practice of Teaching* (1883):

Glory to the strong on the reverse side of the shield is oppression to the weak. The weak are pushed into a corner and neglected; their natural tendency to shrink from labour is educated into despair, by their being constantly reminded, directly or indirectly, that their labour is no good. . . The pride of intellect is to be unchained and with the break up of humility, reverence and holiness . . . the Darker Age will set in to be wondered at in turn in years to come. There is to be no room for the weak.

This statement, so appropriate to our time, was written nearly a century ago.

6

Pressures of Society on our Schools

It is one of the inevitable facts of our society that each generation of adults puts pressure which may be good or bad on the schools as they educate the generation which is to follow. These pressures may be exerted by governments, by local authorities, by industry, by parents, by the attitudes of the general public and by many other bodies. When the pressures succeed, the instigators take the credit, when they fail, the schools all too often are blamed.

We have no difficulty in listing the kind of changes which have come about in the last fifty or sixty years, and those of my generation can take pride in the wonders of flight, space travel, surgery, electronics, the reduction of poverty and many other achievements which have undoubtedly been of great benefit throughout the world and which owe much to the education we have provided.

To this list, however, we must add the two bloodiest wars in history, pornography, drugs, violence, kidnappings, muggings and buggings all of which must have some effect on the young of our day. We kill easily by our use of mechanical transport, we gamble on a massive scale, we see corruption in the highest places, we pay high wages to the young and then exploit them commercially, we have invented methods of contraception which have utterly changed the attitude of the oung towards matters of sex; and our current laws on divorce mean that there are far more children than there used to be who do not have two normal parents. We have invented and used the bomb and killed millions in the gas chambers, we know all about lethal bacteria and napalm, and similar devices for killing. This list which the young know of and understand has been made possible only by the education which today's generation of fathers and grandfathers have provided. Do we know what damage all this has done to the young of our day?

There is no difficulty in discovering how governments and political parties exert pressures. The happenings of our own day and of the immediate past afford many powerful examples. In my grandfather's time the great debate was whether there should be a public elementary-school system paid for by the public, and there were those who said that to do this would be to put the torch of knowledge in the hands of rick-burners. In my father's time the main debate was whether local rates should be spent on Church schools. It is difficult for us to realize the intensity of the feelings that these relatively recent debates and enactments aroused. Both my grandfathers refused to pay their rates and both of them had visits from the bailiffs who distrained some of their property in order to collect what they owed. In our day we have had and are still having a similar but much less acrimonious debate on comprehensive schools, but governmental pressure in this case has been far less than it was in 1870 or 1902.

It is, however, possible to find instances where successive governments have brought to bear on the young pressures which are still having effects which may yet bring us near to disaster. For instance, as early as the 1840s the Factory Acts contained provisions designed to train and educate the young who were employed in the factories, and in 1843 the Admiralty actually established a School for Dockyard Apprentices. The hope of the day was that this practice would spread but it did not do so and in 1909 the Board of Education Consultative Committee sought to introduce compulsory part-time education for all youngsters up to the age of seventeen, but this too failed. Some years later a departmental committee urged that the juvenile at school should be seen not so much as a little wage earner but as a workman and citizen in training; but little happened and in 1918 the Fisher Acts which proposed to establish Day Continuation Schools also failed. The idea was revived in 1944 when the Butler Act proposed that we should establish County Colleges to accommodate youngsters compulsorily released by industry. This idea was taken up by the Crowther Committee in 1959, who devoted a whole section of their report to it but with very little result. We now have thousands of teenage youngsters unemployed and often ill-educated and ill-prepared for what is going to happen to them. We have established the Manpower Services Commission which is doing its best to help, and short-term periods of employment by means of job creation are being operated all over the country. But the striking fact of all this is that for over a century governments have time and again tried and failed to help those youngsters who have been left over after the scholars and the skilled have been provided for.

National attitudes and industrial pressures have forced the schools to play their part in this sad story. Ever since we agreed as a nation to provide secondary education, our aim has been to 'pick out the best' and apply our energies and our resources to them. This was tolerable when those who were not selected constituted 80 per cent or more of the population but now that we are selecting more and more for some kind of continued education those who are passed over are likely to become a festering group in our society. The schools are still pressurized to deal with the gifted and with those whom compassion determines should be given remedial help, but the middle group are often neglected. The creation of comprehensive schools has to some extent aggravated this situation. But as I have just said these schools in order to justify themselves have tended to concentrate on their gifted pupils in order to demonstrate that they can do as much for them as the grammar schools used to do. Furthermore, in some schools the slower youngsters find themselves in the eighth or ninth stream of a

ten-form-entry comprehensive school rather than the fourth
stream of a secondary modern, and when the comprehensive
school is a poor one their sense of rejection is intense. The
result of all this is that the schools are in some instances
contributing to a century-old neglect of a whole sector of our
teenage community, and as machines and computers more
and more undertake the work that these youngsters once did
the problem grows graver and graver and the schools will take
more and more of the blame which should be attributed to
successive governments.

The recently developed policy of admitting blacks into our
community will not ease this problem and if we do not tackle it
there will be black children of high ability who fail to get jobs
because white prejudice is against them and they will be bitterly resentful. There will also be black children who are so dull
that they will have no chance of securing jobs when in competition with abler whites and in self-defence they will claim
that it is white prejudice against their colour which is holding
them back. There will also be cases where white children of
low ability will fail to secure jobs when in competition with
abler blacks and this is likely to make the less able whites
dangerously resentful. All these possibilities are creating new
and difficult pressures on our schools which again will be
blamed if and when governments, either local or central, fail
or are weak in their task.

Perhaps the most sinister aspect of our present situation is
that we may be forcing youngsters to take pride in the fact that
they have no job. Status and self-esteem may have to be built
up on the length of time one can spend out of work. It is now
some eight years since I asked a fifteen-year-old what he was
going to do when he left school and he immediately answered,
'Nowt, like me dad.' In more recent years there has developed
a situation in which thousands of our teenaged unemployed
may have been forced to take this view.

At the other end of the ability range we seem to be making
errors which are equally grave and which will in some way or
other reflect on our schools. We are selecting more and more

youngsters for higher education and when they have completed their first or second or even third degree (which costs the public a vast amount of money) they find no job which seems to match their attainments. Moreover, they see that the ever-increasing demand for machines, which diminish the demand for manpower, is going to aggravate their problem. They, more than the older generation and the unskilled, see that the aim of our civilization is material wealth rather than human happiness and dignity. Thus it is that our society is exerting pressure at both ends of the ability range and as things go wrong so the schools will be held to blame. There are, of course, those who believe that in our nascent concern for the slow we are already sacrificing the quick.

I can only quote some of the figures which were revealed in the large Authority for which I worked between 1954 and 1974. During that time students in colleges of education increased by 399.6 per cent, students at the universities by 464 per cent, full-time students in further education by 1908 per cent and part-time students in further education by 1268.2 per cent. I have no reason to doubt that figures from other Authorities would be comparable. These increases were, of course, accommodated by the increase over those years in our universities, polytechnics and technical colleges. What I very much doubt is whether similar increases were produced which have in any way helped the failure layer to which I have referred.

The creation of this layer is perpetual in our schools. The way we create it is seen most easily in the gymnasium. If we are still old-fashioned enough to line up a whole class before a vaulting horse and demand that they vault over it in a certain way which the teacher prescribes, what happens? The first gifted half dozen or so meet the demand with distinction and the teacher enjoys the credit for this. The middle group are less successful but there is some improvement. The last half dozen or so have then to expose their incompetence before the whole class and they often develop a life-long loathing for the whole activity unless of course any of them are defective, in which case they will attract a redeeming pity. And so it is throughout the service. The national attitude is that in the nation's interest the gifted matter, the defective merit our compassion, but those who are normal but slow and dull are of little account. There is another reason why this group is neglected. No teacher has ever been drawn from it and none knows the effects on individual morale of perpetual failure. We have virtually discarded the principle that Carlyle expressed when he said that 'the great law of culture is that each should become all that he was created capable of being.'

There are many other pressures and practices of our society which affect the schools, apart from those of government, either central or local. For instance, there were in 1970 71,000 children under sixteen born of divorced parents; by 1975 this figure had increased to 145,000 and our attitudes to abortion and divorce, whether they be morally right or wrong, are not going to make life easier for the teacher. The adult generation of today has been responsible for tolerating and peddling pornography and drugs, for a great increase in gambling and drink and other dubious developments which cannot fail to influence the young, but when the young are influenced it is they rather than the older generation who are blamed by the adult instigators. We are, so say the older generation, too permissive, but they do not ask who are the permitters and what kind of education created them, neither do they see adult and parental permissiveness as an additional pressure with which the schools have to contend.

There are other adult practices which damage and corrupt the young. Fagin would have had a far easier job today than he did in the days when Dickens invented him. The supermarket is a training ground for thieves, and when the young succumb it is inevitable that the schools are charged with some of the blame. Moreover, we now pay children in their teens considerable sums in a variety of ways and exploit them commercially as never before and this does not make them easier for the schools to handle.

Then there are inventions such as radio and television which have in so many ways been such a boon to education. The sinister fact is, however, that they give instruction in the techniques of villainy and they exploit vandalism and violence and sex before the young in ways which are more intense than can ever have been the case in the past. Furthermore, it must be that what the young see and the frequency with which they see it will mean that they are no longer shocked by what should be shocking. I am, of course, aware that there are those who demand measurable evidence of this. My answer to them is that if firms find it commercially worth while to spend millions of pounds to persuade us to buy this and that and we are in fact persuaded, it is difficult to believe that the young are unaffected by similar intense repetitions of violence and sex.

The media exert pressures on the schools in other ways. Teachers of infants tell me that more and more young children are coming to school having had a dangerously minimal experience of conversation with adults. The bad old saying that 'children should be seen and not heard' has been replaced by one which demands that they should 'shut up while the telly is on' and in some homes this means, of course, all the time. Furthermore, as children only spend six hours or so a day for 200 days in the year at school some will spend almost this length of time before the television screen over the 365 days of each calendar year. There are, of course, pressures brought to bear on the schools by the domestic circumstances of the children they teach and by the policies which local authorities adopt.

We now know from the researches of the National Children's Bureau and others how great are the difficulties of schools which draw their children mainly from overcrowded homes, from homes which lack amenities, from large families, from families of unskilled workers, from single child and single parent families, and from slum areas. We are at last trying to give schools in difficult areas special help but the public at large is still all too ready to compare their achievements and results to their disadvantage with schools which have a much easier task.

In addition to all these grave difficulties which our schools have to surmount, there are those which are more trivial but which arise daily in every school and which were so admirably illustrated by Miss Huxstep, a distinguished headmistress of Chislehurst County Grammar School, when she addressed the North of England Education Conference in 1956. This is how she put it.

In considering how to prepare children for society, we are, it seems, faced by a dilemma, for what society asks of us, and what we think we ought to be doing in our schools are not always the same thing. What preparation does society want from the schools for its children? There is no answer for society does not speak about this matter with one voice but with many. If we try to tune in to its demands we hear a confusing clamour of voices.

'At least 5 subjects at the 'O' level including two sciences.'

'A GCE is no use to me, I want a boy who knows how to write a legible hand, spell correctly and do as he's told.'

'The mid-day meal affords an excellent opportunity for social training.'

'They should all receive sex instruction, mere biology isn't enough.'

'Why don't the schools teach them to speak properly.'

'The future of the world depends on international understanding, so organize journeys abroad. They can be paid for from the profits of the school tuck shop or the proceeds of the school play.'

'I wish you would speak to her, she would take more notice of you.'

'Thrift is a vital national interest and should be encouraged by the formation of a savings group in every school.'

'No one's education is complete unless he can read a railway timetable, follow a church service, has done a small piece of scientific research, has learned Latin and can swim, cook and mend a fuse.'

'I didn't send my girl here to learn to cook, her mother can teach her that at home.'

'Road safety is important for the survival of this nation. Sergeant Brown would be glad to talk to the whole school, inspect the cycles and give a road safety demonstration every term. Alderman Smith has promised a prize for the best poster. Councillor

Jones will give a cup for the best essay.'
'Mother goes out to work and I have to do the shopping, would you mind the money for me.'
'Every child should have the chance to learn to play a musical instrument.'
'Never mind the frills, teach them to spell.'
'A quiet room and supervision should be provided at school for homework.'
'It is not fair to expect a child to concentrate on his homework with the television on.'
'She's thoroughly out of hand, it's time she went to school.'
'What proportion of your children drink milk?'
'What! you haven't a parent-teacher association!'

These then are the kind of matters which any head has to face on every school day, but the final and perhaps the most powerful pressure of all which the schools have to face is that which they have brought on themselves. I refer, of course, to the external examination which I have mentioned but which merits special consideration.

We have a vast machinery for examining in this country on which we probably spend well over £20 million each year quite apart from the teachers' time which the examinations consume. There is no doubt about the control which the examinations exert and this control is in many instances beneficial; indeed, many schools would be in difficulty if it were not there. But the system can also have its dire effects and it is as well that these continue to be discussed.

The main objective of the external examination is to enable us to grade children according to their ability and achievement so that those deemed worthy of continued education can be provided with it. Along with the process of selecting the successful goes, of course, that of rejecting the failures. Another purpose is to ensure that as many children as possible absorb what is deemed to be the measure of knowledge appropriate to their age and ability and a third objective is to ensure that teachers are rendered accountable for seeing to it that those whom they teach reach appropriate and sometimes prescribed standards.

We always have graded our children in this way. When the service started children were grouped not by age but by the standard of their attainment. Every child whatever his age who could 'read a short paragraph from a book not confined to words of one syllable' and who could manage 'to add and subtract numbers of not more than four digits' was placed in Standard I and if those so placed could not manage these tasks when questioned by HMI the school received no money in respect of their education from the government of the day. We have progressed from this elementary beginning through the County Minor Scholarship, the 11 plus, the School Certificate, the CSE, the 'O' level and 'A' level, to our present position, and it is very largely these examinations, particularly at the secondary stage, which determine what we teach.

What are the anxieties to which our examinations give rise? In 1955 the Minister issued a Circular to LEAs which contained the following strong and positive statements.

All examinations restrict to some extent the teacher's freedom. . .

An examination on a national basis for Modern Schools would induce uniformity of syllabuses and curricula and methods at stages and ages where uniformity would be most undesirable. . .

There is a risk that the examinations would be regarded as an index of efficiency in schools. . .

For these and other reasons the Minister decided that 'he does not favour the establishment of any new general examination of national standing for secondary schools.'

However, the Association of Education Committees and the NUT did not see eye-to-eye with these views and they combined in order to induce the Minister of Education to reverse his decision and a national committee under the Chairmanship of Mr Robert Beloe was set up in order to look into the possibility of doing this.

Before the committee reported Chief Education Officers in

Yorkshire received this extraordinary and prophetic letter.

> The General Certificate & the Picture
> Framers Union,
> Clapham Hall,
> Equity Street,
> London S.W.1.

Dear Sirs,

Secondary School Examinations

I am instructed by my Executive to appeal for your support. My union believes there should be a secondary school examination for all children according to their age, ability and aptitudes. At the present time the GCE is the only examination recognized at national level. This means that secondary modern school children are placed at a disadvantage. Employers are beginning to look at the General Certificate obtained by some of these children and when they see they have only passed in one subject, perhaps Needlework or Religious Instruction, they make sarcastic or sardonic remarks to the children. This, of course, hurts their egos and your Association will be aware that psychologists say there is nothing so wounding to a young worker as to have his ego hurt.

To deal with this serious matter we propose there shall be a series of secondary school examinations at all levels so graduated that every child shall pass in 5 subjects. Under our scheme there would be a 1st class certificate, a 2nd class certificate and a 3rd class certificate, and so on, down to children in the Educationally Subnormal Schools who should, we believe, qualify for a 'Highly Delighted'. Once this system is established we can subsequently succeed to eliminate class.

You will see, therefore, that every child would get a certificate with 5 passes which he would be able to have framed by a member of our union.

We appeal to you to give us your help in our campaign for justice to every child. Give us a free hand and we will soon make all children equal, subject to the maintenance of the appropriate pay differentials.

> Yours fraternally,
>
> W. Hall
> General Secretary

This we soon discovered was written by Frank Barraclough, the Director of Education of the North Riding, as it was in those days. The fascinating feature of this letter is that it was written before the publication of the national report which eventually introduced the CSE grades which were not unlike those which Barraclough forecast.

The nub of the whole letter is the sarcastic promise to make children equal. The whole examination system tends to overlook the variables which inevitably make examining unreliable. It is as if we were deliberately blind to the forces which can make children of similar ability produce such different results at a given test. What we are trying to find out is how they vary in their ability to master the knowledge which they have gained. What we tend to overlook is the extent to which such assessments elude us because the candidates can vary from the permanently sick to the abundantly healthy. They vary in their homes from the shack to the utterly comfortable. They vary in social background from the industrial slum to the exclusive suburb. They vary from the almost incomprehensible to the brilliantly articulate. They vary from the child who is loved at home to the child who is completely unwanted. They vary in their resilience from the over aggressive to the sadly withdrawn, and this list could, of course, be vastly extended.

But the variations are not confined to the home. Though the differences between school and school are nothing like as great as those between home and home they nevertheless exist and extend from the near miraculous to the lamentably weak. Inside the schools the children vary from the way they attract or repel the teacher and the way they are attracted or repelled by him. They vary in their sensitivity, their energy, their confidence and in many other personal qualities which affect their learning.

Finally, of course, the subjects which the children take vary in their measurability from two plus two to the sensitive assessment of a poem or a painting or a musical rendering. Inevitably there are some subjects the marking of which will be subject to the idiosyncrasies of the marker despite all the admirable and thorough attempts of the examining boards to avoid variations arising from such a source.

It is because of these and other variables that the examinations are and always will be to some extent unreliable, and it is nonsense ever to talk of equality of opportunity or of a borderline when the best we can ever hope to achieve is a border land.

I recall without effort the occasions in my own experience which have led me to realize how unreliable examinations can be. As a young teacher I taught to defeat the examiner and in a very weak class secured twenty-three School Certificate passes out of twenty-seven. As I went round the staffroom making modest noises of astonishment at my success I so well remember the ablest teacher on the staff saying to me, 'You do realize don't you Clegg that in any sensible system you would get the sack for that result.' I protested and he then asked me how many I thought should have passed and I replied, 'About a dozen'. He then pointed out that I had taught not as I believed I should have taught but to defeat the examiner.

In the course of my career as an Education Officer I time and again came across occasions which proved how devastatingly wrong results can be. My first shock came when I asked the HMI responsible for the statistics of the Central Advisory Committee reports what degree of error I should be likely to make when selecting twenty children out of 100 for a grammar-school education. His answer was 10 per cent to 15 per cent and when I asked him if this meant that for every twenty eventually chosen for the grammar school I might, judging by subsequent performance, select at least half a dozen who should not have been selected and fail to select half a dozen who should, he confirmed this point.

I recall another incident which added to my doubts. When the Don Valley Comprehensive High School was opened the first intake included sixty-four children who had 'failed' the 11 plus test the year before. Those failures were put through a shortened GCE course to 'O' level at which exam thirty-one secured at least five passes and twenty-two went on to take 'A' levels and proceed to university or college courses. I also remember the embarrassing successes obtained by a primary-school teacher, Mrs Pyrah, whose unusual techniques of developing the speech and confidence of the children led to them securing more than twice the number of 11 plus successes that experience had led us to expect.

Then there were the notorious 'O' level results at Otley Grammar School. In 1964 the headmaster put in twenty-eight pupils for the English Language paper at the 'O' level with two different Boards. These were not borderline candidates, but one Board passed twenty-seven and failed one while the other passed three and failed twenty-five. Under one Board the average grade was four, under the other it was eight. Two candidates only out of twenty-eight were placed in the same grade by both Boards and one candidate was placed in the top grade by one Board and the bottom grade by the other. There have been reports of similar 'experiments' in the press and two major suggestions have been made: one is so to synchronize the exams of the different Boards that this kind of thing cannot happen, the other to have one examination Board for the whole country. This, so it seems to me, is tantamount to saying, 'Let us so arrange things that faults cannot be detected,' and 'Let us so arrange things that faults are distributed over the whole country.'

The extent of the error at 11 plus was put in these terms in a county report which was written just before the comprehensive schemes got under way.

It is interesting to observe that if the contentions of the experts are correct, the number of children 'wrongly' placed in our West Riding modern schools would each year fill the places available for first year pupils in ten two form entry Grammar Schools.

There are a number of serious defects in the education system caused by our examinations. They give us an unreliable judgement of many of our children, they lead us to overrate those aspects of the curriculum which are susceptible to measurement and underrate those which are not, they tend to make us distort non-measurable subjects in order to make them measurable and examinable, they are costly, they lead to undesirable competition between child and child, teacher and teacher, school and school. In the last resort they cannot reveal professional potential. A law degree does not reveal the capacity to plead, a medical degree the capacity to care or the teaching qualification the capacity to stimulate the desire to learn.

Having raised all these objections to and criticisms of examinations one has to admit that they are likely to stay and that in the process of assessing standards and making a selection of pupils they make what is probably the best of a bad job. My own view about them is that if they remain they should be more teacher controlled than they now are. I have seen three types of teacher controlled examinations working successfully.

The first was an attempt to cut out the malevolent pressures of the 11 plus by leaving the selection to the schools and equating the schools' judgement by comparing their borderline groups. Of this system the Plowden Report (1967) wrote:

An initial quota of selective places is given to each primary school and is generally based on the results of the previous 3 years. The accuracy of this figure for the current year is checked by a careful investigation of all borderline pupils undertaken by a panel of headteachers. A further check is provided by a feed back of information from the secondary schools to the primary schools. The purpose of this system is to avoid distortion of the primary school curriculum by dispensing with an externally imposed test. It achieves this object without loss of accuracy. It is acceptable to parents and teachers and has led to co-operation between primary and secondary schools. We are impressed by its advantages. . .

This Thorne scheme, as it was called because it was first tried out in the Thorne area near Doncaster, left the 11 plus selection firmly in the hands of the teachers.

A similar step was then taken in the early sixties with the sixteen-year-olds and it became known nationally as Mode Three of the CSE. Groups of twenty or so schools came together to organize the examination. For each subject a panel of teachers was selected, syllabuses were prepared and the schools either followed the prepared syllabus or submitted ones which they had drawn up. In an endeavour to achieve uniformity of assessment there were assessment trials at which potential assessors each graded the same set of scripts. The schools then did their own subject to this being validated by an assessor from another school. The great advantage of this scheme was that individual teachers could use subject material which they deemed appropriate to their pupils.

A scheme was next devised which placed a part of university selection firmly in the hands of the Authority. It arose from the fact that youngsters in the South Yorkshire coalfield were not getting the admissions to Oxbridge which statistically they ought to have had. Three colleges in Oxford and three in Cambridge agreed to participate in an experiment. The Authority selected pupils from their sixth forms before they took their 'A' levels and many of these youngsters were chosen deliberately from a working–class background of the kind that the Robbins report had stated was not producing university candidates in numbers proportionate to the ability of the group.

The Authority endeavoured to ensure that each pupil selected should take his 'A' levels and then spend a year in industry or in voluntary service of some kind before taking his place at the university. Firms of national repute such as ICI, David Brown, Rolls Royce, Boots and others took some of the pupils while others did voluntary service in Kano, Zambia, Honduras, Algeria and other parts of the world. One did scientific research in Miami and two worked on a bridge that was being built in Israel. This scheme lasted several years and the academic results were well above the county average. No pupils failed though one withdrew from the scheme. Many achieved athletic and other distinctions in their colleges.

The point of mentioning these three schemes is to show that at each stage, 11 plus, 'O' level, and university entrance, the selection of youngsters could be left to the teachers who see them day in and day out. Such a step would give much freedom to the schools and it is doubtful whether the errors in selection would be any greater than those which are inevitable in any system of external examining. There is one other point which should be emphasized: there is not the slightest doubt that getting these youngsters into work between school and university was in most cases of the utmost value. It gave them social confidence and rubbed off a number of otherwise impeding corners. It would in my view be worthwhile considering this on a much wider scale.

It is experiences such as these with pupils of varying ages which make me hope that the teaching professions will undertake a professional responsibility which is properly theirs rather than continue to hire external examiners, checkers, assessors and testers as if the teachers themselves were not to be trusted. A. N. Whitehead put this view in *The Aims of Education* (1929):

In education as elsewhere the broad primrose path leads to a nasty place. This evil path is represented by a book or set of lectures which will practically enable the student to learn by heart all the questions likely to be asked at the next external examination, and I may say in passing that no external system is possible unless every question directly asked of the pupil at any examination is either framed or modified by the actual teacher of that pupil in that subject.

More recently the late Christian Schiller, HMI, when he was responsible for the country's junior schools, wrote this to me about the 11 plus test and similar tests designed to compare child with child.

To expect boys and girls who pass at a set time each year into secondary schools to line up level along a tape in respect of any characteristic or attainment is to be blind to the way the Creator has chosen to make our world. What can be accomplished by a boy who when he leaves the primary school has a mental age of 11 is far beyond the powers of a boy or girl whose mental age at that time is only 9 or 10.

If a minimum of attainment is fixed such that it is within the powers of all it is demonstrably irrelevant to the vast majority and of no practical value. If a minimum is fixed such that some only can reach it, it must be demonstrably beyond the powers of the rest and its imposition will undoubtedly lead to the distortion of those powers. In my opinion the goal of a minimum of attainment is incompatible with continuity in the process of learning.

What Schiller overlooks in his statement is the fact which is obvious but which we all are reluctant to admit, namely, that the standardized attainment test is used as a means of checking the ability of the teachers.

But the main case against the grading of children was put the best part of a century ago by Edward Thring in *Theory and Practice of Teaching* in these terms:

There is a prescribed packet to be learned and if a boy does not learn it, it is no business of the clerk of works (the teacher) beyond punishing him for not doing it. This soon passes into a neglect of those who cannot, or will not, pigeonhole the daily quota, this naturally advances to finding them very much in the way; the next step is that in the interest of the better boys (so runs the story) they must be got rid of. So the school failures are turned out and great authority quoted to support the practice: and all the energy of the place is expended on the strong and active who will distinguish themselves in the knowledge scramble.

In the future the examination pressure is likely to become increasingly controversial. If we are going to have an almost permanent layer of young unemployed in our society how sensible is it to demand that they should all learn the details of the battle of Waterloo even if the external examiners believe this to be essential?

PART II
People

7

Children

When I first began to work in education administration, those of us on the inside of the service held a number of fairly simple beliefs about the children in our schools. They were born with a certain ability and this we could measure with an intelligence test. We could then with reasonable certainty pick out the ablest children and give them an education which accorded with their age, aptitude and ability. So we tested them all at the age of eleven, we put the clever ones in the grammar schools, the next layer in many areas found their way into junior technical or junior art schools, and the rest went to such all-age schools as still remained, or into modern schools.

I was in Birmingham at the time, and we accepted the fact that there would be far fewer clever children from the poorer areas of Rae Street and Steward Street than from Harborne where those who were clever and wealthy lived. It was as simple as that, and we made the assumption, even if we did not state it, that the shortcomings of the Steward Street children were inherited, and to some extent this was true.

But in those days, few of us realized, as now we do, how long is the list of impediments which can contribute to the insecurity and lack of confidence and of achievement of those children who live in the grey areas of the country, where housing is dismal and amenities are poor. As teachers in training we had learned academically from Percy Nunn about horme and mneme, about routine and ritual, about the play-

way and so on. As teachers in employment we had made a
profound study of examination questions and how to coach
our pupils in the art and science of answering them. We were
not anything like as fully aware, as we now are, of the long list
of differences between education in 'Smogville' and the education in 'Cheltenmouth'.

Today however, because of the researches of the National
Children's Bureau and of many other individuals and bodies, as
well as discoveries of several Central Advisory Councils, we
know much more about these differences. We know, for
instance, that in the grey areas:

more children die young
more children suffer ill health
more have sick parents
more live in areas where doctors are scarce
more have parents who depend to some extent on their children's
earnings
more live in overcrowded homes
more live in homes which lack the basic amenities
more have parents who are school shy
more have parents who left school as soon as they were able
more are dependent on the social services
more have come into contact with the probation service and with
detention
more live in an area where there is dirt and pollution
more live in ugly derelict areas
more attend old and ill-kept schools which are awaiting closure
more come from homes where books are few
more are taught by teachers who do not live in the area
more are from impoverished families
more are from families dependent on school meals
more lack the facilities necessary to keep themselves clean
fewer have parents who know their way about the education service
fewer hear school English spoken in their homes
fewer talk often with adults
fewer read to their parents
fewer have parents who read to them
fewer have articulate parents

fewer receive extra–curricular help
fewer take enriching holidays
fewer are taken to galleries or concerts by their parents
fewer question their parents about school matters
fewer have parents who could answer questions about school matters if asked
fewer become prefects
fewer are members of school teams
fewer join youth clubs
fewer stay at school beyond the leaving age
fewer experience success at school
fewer take external examinations
fewer succeed in those examinations when they take them
fewer obtain jobs immediately on leaving school.

The National Children's Bureau has shown us how potent these social impediments to learning can be. Children from large families are likely to be twelve months behind in their reading at the age of seven, children from homes with poor amenities eight months behind, children of parents who left school as soon as they legally could six months per parent behind, and the difference between the children of unskilled workers and those of the top professionals is a gap of seventeen months. It is curious that for so long we have failed to assess the full effect of environment, yet it is probably true to say that however stupid, no farmer on earth who had ten cows on scrub land and ten cows on good pasture would attribute the difference in milk yield to inheritance. There is of course no doubt about the factor of inheritance, but it is significant that when Dr Pringle looked at the performance of seriously deprived children, the illegitimate group, she found that they rose from a position well below average to a position above it once they had been taken into caring homes.

Fortunately most children are resilient and most can survive combinations of most damaging circumstances. But the heads and teachers of schools which serve the more dismal social areas are fully aware of the symptoms and effects of domestic deprivation on the less resilient of their pupils. There are children who are denied attention at home and overtly crave it in school, children who have learned cruelty and viciousness at home and are cruel and vicious in school; children who, because they are repellent, are rejected by their peers and crave the constant support of the teacher, or who are defiant and aggressive in order to secure in one way the attention they do not easily get in another, children who are fearful and withdrawn, and the list could be greatly extended.

There are those who claim that such children are exceptional, but in fact they are to be found in every classroom in existence, for in any group of children there will be one who is the least happy, one who is the least loved, one who is the least likeable, one who is the least articulate and so on. It should not of course be thought that children born into affluence and comfort do not from time to time also suffer. Indeed one of the worst fates that can befall a pupil of modest ability is to be the offspring of ambitious parents whose pressures are such that they are likely to give the child a loathing of the whole school learning process. And of course there are now many homes where children are given such lavish attention that they are insulated against the school's endeavours to stimulate, they become blasé, and what the teacher does to enliven learning is no more than tolerated.

There are politicians who believe that putting all children in the same comprehensive school will somehow or other remove these differences which are brought about by differing social and domestic circumstances. What is not fully realized is that birds of a feather will tend to flock together even when put in an aviary with other birds. And to continue the metaphor, there are certain birds with so much oil on their wings that it can only be removed by the most specific attention and the use of plentiful and costly resources.

An area which I know well, the Harewood Centre in Pontefract, which is directed by Miss Lesley Kissack, does more for the children who need help than any other place of its kind that I know. It has a nursery school attended during the day by two separate groups and the mothers come in until the children are 'settled', which means that many become active voluntary helpers. There are also two youth groups, one for children of five to eleven years of age who meet after school, and one for children of eleven plus who meet in the evenings, so that the Centre's care for children is continuous. The Centre also offers valuable help to a group that is difficult to control and consists of the least manageable youngsters from the local secondary schools. During the week there are also social and recreational meetings for parents. But one of the significant features about this venture, which is in a relatively stable area, is that the teacher-social-worker or liaison-teacher as we called him, has dealt with some six hundred cases in four years. All these children need special support, just as much as do those children in schools for the handicapped. Miss Kissack's plea is that they be treated with consistent care in school to make up for the uncertainty of their life when out of it. There should be, she claims, some caring but unsentimental adult who is as continuously as possible available to them, and this person should be one who respects the youngsters and is respected by them, someone who can offer them individual attention and understanding and who knows how best to continue to succeed in a way that will build their self-realization and self-esteem, and stimulate their further endeavours.

She claims also that the physical provision for such children is important. They need somewhere where they can play out their aggression in physical activity but also a place for quiet relaxation, a place for fun and laughter and a place where they will make contact with beauty in its many forms. In difficult areas she would prefer a centre which is separate from the school they attend, in order to make certain that there is no conflict of purpose or of standards. If such a place could not be found, then of course provision should be made in the school.

Centres of this kind reveal individual items of deprivation which can all too readily hold a child back. In many parts of the country and in South Yorkshire in particular the speech of the background area into which the child is born can impede his progress. A year or two ago a list of vernacular expressions which circulated in the South Yorkshire schools made this problem lightheartedly specific. The list included the following phonetic phrases:

gerritetten
smarrerweeim
azeegeniter
isthemum
weve gorra gerrus imbux
asta gorrit withy
tintintin
gerrarry tegithi andweeit
ee sez ee antadit
lerrer geront bus
ayampteared nowt

In many parts of this country and certainly in English-speaking countries such as Australia and the USA these phrases are incomprehensible, but they are common enough in South Yorkshire and well into Derbyshire. The important thing as far as the schools are concerned is that children who start their speaking in this way will have to able to translate 'oowurreewee' into 'who was he with' before they can begin to write and spell. It is futile for ardent dialecticians or those who resent the connection between class and speech to protest that the schools are imposing a middle-class language on their children. The simple fact is that in order to master writing and reading, the child must become familiar with the normal spoken language. For many schools this is a serious and exacting task and it is one in which the best schools engage the help of parents, even to the extent of providing classes for parents on how best to help their children and how to make sure that the children enjoy their learning.

The need for the enjoyment is often sadly overlooked. Most of us who have had the good fortune to be able to advance in our education have been able to discard those aspects of it which we disliked. Those who have learned more slowly have not had this advantage, and many have grown up with a loathing of ill-taught skills. The slower the child is, the more important it will be that he should achieve the kind of success on which self-esteem can be built. The importance of the joy in learning has been driven home time and time again by our great educators. Ascham, in *On Education* (1711) quotes Socrates on this point: 'No learning ought to be learned with bondage, for bodily labours hurt not the body but any learning learned by compulsion tarrieth not in the mind.' Locke in *Some Thoughts Concerning Education* (1693) is equally specific:

The right Way to teach these Things is to give them a Liking and Inclination to what you propose to them to be learned and that will engage their Industry and Application. . . Thus much for learning to read which let him never be driven to nor chid for; cheat him into it if you can but make it not a Business for him! tis better it be a Year later before he can read than that he should in this way get an Aversion to Learning.

As a nation we are still a little resistant to the idea that learning should be enjoyed. Life is severe, we say, and children must be made aware of this and of their own shortcomings. School should make them face what is unpleasant. Edward Thring described this theory in these terms: 'There is a fearful theory born and bred in the quagmires of Marsh-Dunceland, that nothing is worth learning unless it is disagreeable, or worth having unless it is difficult.'

The need for children, and particularly the slow-learning children, to enjoy what they learn, is perhaps more important now than ever it has been. If, as seems likely, a relatively small fraction of our society is going to be able to produce the materials that life demands, we shall have to ask ourselves much more earnestly than we have done in the past, 'What are we educating our children for?'

The easy answer is that we are educating them in order that they may make wise use of their leisure, when, as seems likely to happen, the working week and the working day are reduced and holidays are increased. But the kind of leisure which we shall have to prepare youngsters for is that which will give them some satisfaction and self-realization. If we do not do this, but thoughtlessly train them for careers which are going to be closed to them, or for work which will not exist, we must prepare for the explicable villainy which will ensue.

We have reached a stage in our civilization when we see with what disastrous force damaging conditions and circumstances can afflict the personalities of the young. The nettle we have not yet fully grasped is that these damaging pressures exerted steadfastly on a youngster during the early years of his life can and frequently do turn those who lack resiliance into vicious and dangerous members of our society. And all too often we then blame them for what is our responsibility and for what adult society has brought about.

There is however another nettle which will become increasingly troublesome if it is not dealt with. In recent years all in the service of education have learned of the ways in which bad social conditions can harm the learning process. One of the side effects of this realization is that weak teachers and even weak heads and weak schools are tending to excuse their weaknesses by laying the blame for them, not on their own incompetence, but on what we now call 'deprivation'. This is likely to be an increasing danger, and one which Authorities, through their Inspectors and Advisers, will have to be fully aware of.

Teachers

I suppose most of us in our youth came into contact with the normal categories of teacher. If we were lucky we were taught by teachers from whom we learned with enjoyment. We were almost certainly taught by some who compelled us to learn. Then there were those from whom we learned little and at worst those who gave us a positive distaste for what they were trying to make us learn.

The teachers who gave us delight would be those who had realized that for any good teacher the raw material is the mind, body and spirit of his pupil, for these are what he will cultivate and nourish and for him subjects and drills and experiences are but the nutrients. For the teacher who makes the child learn we must change the metaphor. He fills the mind but does not necessarily kindle the fire which will illuminate it over a life-time. The teacher who creates a distaste is unfortunately none too rare; in fact my experience leads me to believe that most of us have acquired a permanent distaste for some subject or other because of the way it was taught to us or because of the personality of the teacher who taught it.

I have not the competence to write a dissertation on teaching as a profession but I have looked with some care at two groups of mainly primary-school teachers who differ considerably in their approach to the job they do. I refer to the teachers whom we label 'formal' or 'traditional' and those to whom we refer as 'informal' or 'progressive' in their technique. What do we mean when we speak of a formal teacher; what does he do and what is he like when he teaches well, and what does he do and what is he like when he teaches badly?

The teacher who leans towards formality in the way he works tends to believe that his main job is to impart knowledge, to inculcate rules of behaviour and to mould character. The unit which he teaches will normally be a group of some thirty or so children and the pace of learning will be determined by the average rate of progress of the group as a whole. The methods he will use will be didactic, his pupils will be 'told' and required to learn, and the basis of the teaching will more often than not be a published syllabus, supported by prescribed textbooks and enlivened by films, film strips, records, tapes and aids of all kinds. But the teacher will also devise his own schemes of work and he will know from experience at what rate he expects his class to progress.

He will exert considerable authority in what he does and the way he does it, he will tend when teaching to assume a dominating position in front of his class as this will facilitate his control over his pupils. The timetable and syllabuses which he has prepared and to which he will work with meticulous care will ensure that his pupils spend what he believes to be the requisite amount of time on each subject. He will use competition as a motive force, believing that those of his pupils who are ahead will want to keep ahead and those who have fallen back will want to catch up. He will set work to the whole class and this he will regularly collect, mark and return to them. He will often impose drills and techniques somewhat before the actual need for them arises, and they will then be used in ways which will prepare his pupils to face the examinations and tests by which most school programmes are controlled.

The good points of his teaching are fairly obvious. His work will be conducted in accordance with well-tried practice and well thought-out schemes. He will present it in doses which he knows to be assimilable and the work of his class will show progress, lesson by lesson, week by week and month by month. He will insist that work is well presented and will do all in his power to ensure that his pupils are interested in what he teaches them. He will know his pupils and their abilities and he will try his best to ensure that they live up to his expectations of them. His standards of discipline will be clear, and he will expect his pupils to be well mannered to him as he is to them. What he does will be well planned, well organized and well run. The work of his pupils will be regularly demanded, regularly presented, regularly marked, and the marks will form the basis of reports regularly sent to parents. The rules on which the school depends will be well understood by his class and he will strive at all times to emphasize the importance of law and order.

But the best of formal teachers will meet with difficulties. When thirty or more pupils are taught the same thing at the same time it is almost inevitable that sometimes the quick have to mark time while the slow struggle to keep up. Sometimes even the best of teachers will make too little allowance for individual differences and when a whole class is being taught as a unit it is not easy for the teacher to contrive success for his slower learners who so much need the impetus which it can give. Again, even the best of teachers can be carried away by the exhilarating success of the gifted and give too little attention to the devastating effects of continued failure on the weak. There is also the temptation to give too much attention to the subject, the nutrient, and too little to whether it is nourishing growth as it should.

The formal teacher is tempted by the meticulous prescription which he follows to emphasize memory and routine at the expense of initiative. Content and imagination, and for him creative powers, often matter far less than form. The teacher, even the very good teacher, may offer constant praise to those who without much effort may 'come top' while those who 'come bottom' have to make do with his pity.

At his worst the formal teacher is a disaster. He uses force and fear because he knows no other way, and his pupils are often fearful and withdrawn or resentfully aggressive. He still acquires books in class sets and insists on their being read chapter by chapter. If he teaches art his pictures are drawn and paintings and models produced almost to command but without forethought, discussion or stimulus. If he teaches mathematics it will often be as a set of ill-understood tricks. Much of his teaching will be from old syllabuses and there will be too much dull and routine textbook learning. He will take the credit for the demonstrable successes of his gifted pupils and blame the poverty of achievement of those who are slow on their dullness. All too often he will demand that the whole class do the same thing at the same time regardless of whether it is right for individual members at their stage of development. He will be unaware of the personal development of his pupils as their marks, on which he so much depends, will not reveal this to him. His pupils will be bored and the aggressive amongst them will fight and bully in the playground, while the fearful will huddle near the doors and walls. At worst there will be indecent insolence and vandalism exerted as a kind of revenge, and at the end of each session pupils will pour out of his classroom in noisy and offensive relief. Thus it is that formal teachers can range from the excellent to the disastrous.

What are informal teachers like at their best and at their worst? The informal teacher sees himself not so much as imparting knowledge but as one whose task is to excite in his pupils the desire to learn, to draw out their latent powers, to nourish their senses, cultivate their attitudes and establish their values.

The unit that the informal teacher teaches will tend to be the individual or the small group more often than the class as a whole, though the good informal teacher will not hesitate to instruct the whole class if in his judgement it is right at any given moment so to do. He will however rely considerably on the child finding out for himself and on learning by what he does in the belief that he is more likely to understand what he actually does. His working position will tend to be amongst the children rather than in front of them and he will allow them to move freely about the classroom in their search for information and help. His pupils will tend to work individually or in small groups but he will have careful methods of recording how much time each child spends on this or that activity or subject. With this reservation every effort will be made to allow the pupil to continue with the work he has on hand for as long as his zest for it lasts.

The teacher will rely less on competition as a motive and more on encouragement provided by work well displayed, in the belief that the bright child will forge ahead in any case, and the weaker one should not be held back by constant reminders that he is failing. The teacher will make every effort to correct work in the presence of the pupil, and drills and techniques will be introduced when the child appreciates the need for them, in the belief that if they are forced upon him when the need is not understood by him they may well produce a distaste for the very thing they are designed to promote and foster. The teacher will be concerned to develop his own powers of observation and his own sensitivity in the belief that this will help him to increase the sensitivity of his pupils' writing and painting and enrich their creative work generally. Work which is the result of special effort will be put on display and given pride of place, especially if it be the work of a less gifted pupil. This use of display will replace the use of the mark list by the more traditional teacher.

Once he is established such a teacher will have few disciplinary problems as his pupils' energies will be absorbed by the work which they do. He will in consequence have little need for punishment. The pupils will talk freely as the occasion demands, but the noise of the classroom will be purposeful. The abler pupils will, as need arises, help those who are less gifted. The teacher will at all times be ready to nourish a child's effort by allowing him considerable choice, but the choice will be made from a range contrived by the teacher who will know the needs of the child at any particular moment in his development. With such a teacher, content will be more important than form, initiative more important than knowledge and responsibility more important than duty.

In such teaching there is a mystery to which I constantly

return. Given the circumstances I have described there will be many children who develop a creative power in a given medium which exceeds anything of which their teacher is capable. I do not of course refer to technique but to the early signs of creative inspiration which in all but the most gifted artists are so often overlaid by technique in their adult performance. The vision of this kind of manifestation of the human spirit can be the most rewarding result of a visit to the classroom of a teacher who uses and believes in informal teaching.

But of course there are teachers who aspire to use informal methods and are bad at it. My former colleague and educational Adviser, Miss Rae Milne, has produced a description which has gained almost national currency of a school where the informal teaching is bad. She says such a school is like 'a wet play-time all day', and another colleague, Mr L. Horner, who was a very distinguished informal teacher before he became a Senior Adviser, has described such a school as one where 'the teachers have climbed on the band-waggon but cannot play the instruments.' The poor informal teacher all too often teaches on 'progressive' lines not out of conviction but because he is determined to be in the van of fashion. He may even withdraw from teaching lest he 'impose' on his pupils. He will rarely be prepared to say 'this is not good enough' and he will not know when to step in and help and when to leave his pupil to find out for himself. His attitude at worst can be grossly over-sentimental. He will show a lack of preparation in his teaching and his recording of progress will be inadequate with the result that he will seldom know whether a child does something better the second time than he does it the first. Progress will be poor and standards low and there will be activity for the sake of activity. If his pupils appear to be busy he will be satisfied, he will replace the valuable idea of freedom for a 'do as you like' attitude which at worst can lead to classroom chaos. The classroom, as a result of the false idea of freedom, will all too often be a mess, which his pupils will not know how to clear up and such display as there is will tend to be too sentimental, too pretty, and have very little motive purpose. His room will be too noisy and will often show a confusion of captions, questions and instructions. The keeping of small livestock will reveal an animal slum, and in his determination to be in fashion the teacher will use a multiplicity of gadgets and manufactured aids which promise almost pre-natal reading. There will be much time spent on word-matching, and on expendable workbooks which demand little more than ticks, crossings out and underlinings. Such writing as there is will be artificially fancy.

If the school is an infant school there will be an abundance of tissue paper screwed into little balls and stuck into outlines drawn by the teacher. Clay, which can be so valuable when well used, will all too readily be little more than rolled sausages or crude little pots. The room will be full of jigsaws and interlocking bricks and the total of such contrivances in use at any time will be more than teacher or pupils can manage.

There are, I believe, certain qualities which exist in any first-class teacher, whether he teach formally or informally. The following are some of these qualities:

He believes that love is a better spur to learning than fear.

He agrees with Montaigne that more often than not 'savoir par coeur n'est pas savoir'.

He believes that the sort of person a child becomes is often more important than what he knows.

He is hesitant about accepting a syllabus of learning prescribed by an examination or devised by a person who has no knowledge of the background of the children in his class.

He tries to ensure that every child has an experience of success and he acclaims this success and tries to build on it.

He knows the lamentable effect on children of incessant failure.

He knows the limitations of trying to measure what a child has learned and he uses measurement with wise discrimination.

He knows and acts on the fact that delight in the performance of a skill is essential to the real mastery of it.

He gives responsibility not only to children who can discharge it but also to children whose development needs this experience.

He knows how to encourage older children to help the young and the strong to help the frail.

He uses knowledge as material for the mind to work on, and not as a lump of matter to be forced into a container.

He understands the very full part that parents can and should play in education and he maintains a fruitful contact with them and often uses them wisely in school.

He knows that there are times when he will be more effective if he works with a group of colleagues than if he works singly.

He knows it is part of his job to cultivate initiative, sensitivity and confidence as well as to impart facts.

He knows what he means by good behaviour and he knows how to secure it from his children.

He knows that knowledge is doubling every decade or so and that the bit of it that he uses to stimulate his children today may be very different from the bits he used five years ago. and the bit he will use five years hence.

He knows that a number of his pupils will follow the educational route which he followed but he is particularly careful to try and understand the hopes and fears, the loves and hates, the enthusiasms and antipathies of youngsters who are far less well endowed than he himself and than the majority of his class.

He knows also that a number of his pupils will have come from homes with very little support and resource and that somehow this will have to be made up to them.

He knows that each child is subject to different pressures and influences and he tries to harness the better pressures to his use and to counteract the bad ones.

In particular he knows of the many ways in which a child can be handicapped and disadvantaged and he does all in his power to help these special cases.

It is still probably true to say that the most important and influential person in the education of our children is the head of the school and I have often discussed with my administrative and advisory colleagues the qualities of a good head.

In the first place he will be concerned about all his pupils and not merely about those who will bring credit to the school. He so arranges things that every child is known intimately to him or to a reliable member of his staff who will have the capacity to help the child with problems and build up his confidence. The head himself will know the value and place of praise and encouragement and he will easily and as a matter of course consult his pupils in much that the school does, and this will be done without condescension. He will give responsibility to those pupils who need to bear it and not merely to those who easily do so. He will be firm but not autocratic and as he goes about his school he will enjoy and be refreshed by seeing good work by both staff and pupils. He will expect from time to time to have to tackle the grimmest personal problems of his staff and it will be known that he will do this with fairness. He will from time to time have to punish and his known sense of justice will enable him to do this without causing undue resentment. His attitude on all occasions will be calm and he will seldom raise his voice and never resort to sarcasm and humiliation.

He will be welcomed in the staffrooms of his school and in talking to his colleagues he will have no hesitation in confessing to his own weaknesses as he admires and encourages their strengths. He will delegate easily as he will know which members of his staff have qualities and expertise which he does not possess. He will keep a watchful eye on his weaker members of staff and strive to strengthen them with the kind of encouragement which he expects they will use in leading their pupils to self-realization. He will make certain that he or some wise experienced members of his staff care for the probationers. His administration, that is to say the routine and mechanical side of it, will be well done but he will know, and he will make sure that his colleagues know, that this in his view is of secondary importance. He will have a clear vision and understanding of the aims of the school which he will have thrashed out with his staff and he will have enough strength to see that these aims do not become too routine. He will know the value and the limitations of academic work and will at the same time have a wise control over the time spent in a staff meeting on such matters as long hair, earrings, uniform and the trivia of fashion. He will have control over his own fears and will be able to help his staff on theirs. The school will be a democratic group in which all who have a place in it, children, teachers, cleaners, meals staff, have a part to play which they know the head will recognize and esteem. Parents will be welcomed in the school which they will be encouraged to see and use as an amenity within the community. They will know that every child matters and that every parent will be listened to with fairness regardless of his social standing.

The building will be well kept as the head will have convinced his staff of the connection between cleanliness, beauty and behaviour. Pictures, flowers and displays of all kinds will play their part in the school but the school will never become a 'show' school in the pejorative sense of the word. The head, whatever his dignity and status, will always find time personally to investigate the intimate recesses of the building. The morning assembly will be a moving occasion in which reverence and the beauty of music and reading will be significant. Children and staff will take part in it and enjoy it.

In a school where these principles and practices obtain the head will be a warm-hearted, caring person who nevertheless knows how to avoid sentimentality. He will be aware of quality and excellence; he will stimulate and encourage and be welcomed in the classrooms. He will have a sense of fun which will help his relationship with both pupils and staff colleagues, and he will know the value of enjoyment in learning.

In short, the good head is a person with an unsentimental love of children who is specially concerned with the less fortunate. He can win over pupils and staff and kindle a spark in them; he knows the school's aims and sees to it that all the school's activities contribute to those aims and he can distinguish between sterile and fruitful work. He can manage the administration of the school without forsaking the substance of headmastering for the shadow of management.

The poor head lacks many of these qualities. He is unaware of much that goes on in his school because he is glued to his office desk and papers. He tends to see textbooks not as aids but as prescribed syllabuses, though from time to time he will adopt a current fashion. Marks are his motive and examination results provide the status which so matters to him and which he will often shroud in his gown. He will greet visitors from behind his desk. Prestige and status are important to him and he will encourage the conformist and successful but be impatient of the difficult, the distressed and the unusually endowed. He will not be welcome in his staffroom and the politeness to him of staff and pupils if it exists will be artificial.

But the main distinction between the good head and the head who is indifferent or poor is that the former knows the difference between the mind and the spirit and the way each must be nourished to promote the growth of the child.

I have been moved to write personally about my experiences by a statement which Sir Michael Sadler, one of the most notable educationists of his day, wrote about my own father. In this statement written after my father's death, Sadler revealed the qualities which he clearly deemed to be important in the head of a school. These are his words:

Samuel Clegg was an artist, a poet, a radical pioneer, a stringent stimulating teacher, an undaunted soul . . . he had faith and character. His work in school was an intimate echo of his inner life. He loved his fellow men, gave himself generously for others and by losing himself in his appointed task, gained new life and power. . . Nothing but the best he believed was good enough for children and he strove to surround them with beautiful things and create for them an environment that was charged with sweetness and light. He believed that education was much more than success in examinations, though a long list of distinctions proved that the two were not incompatible.

He believed in the fundamental goodness of human nature, in liberty, in gentleness, and in the silent but inevitable influence of cultivated surroundings. . . He was a high voltage cable in a progressive and cordial society, a lover of beauty in literature, art and landscape, an ardent believer in the capacity of almost all minds and hearts to win, in Robert Bridge's words:

New beauty of soul from the embrace of beauty
And strength by practical combat against folly and wrong.

9

Learning to Teach

Student teachers, the colleges they attend and the schools in which they practise, all vary in quality. A potentially good teacher may attend a college which is unduly immersed in the psychology, the philosophy, the sociology and the history of education, but is weak on the all-important techniques of the classroom. He may practise as a student in a school which is sadly out of date, or over-didactic, or merely of poor quality. A teacher in his first post may be given the weakest class in a school which is rigorously streamed, and in which the general belief is that the slowest learners matter least. The effect of a good school on eager students in training can be powerfully beneficial.

A few years ago I was in such a school, and I learned much from a discussion with the probationers and the young teachers working on the staff at that time. I asked a number of them if they would be kind enough to set out briefly their views on their early teaching experiences. This primary school, Balby Street, in the Yorkshire coalfield, then served one of the grimmest areas of back-to-back houses that I have ever known. The homes had few books, the speech in them was not of the kind which the school demanded for its reading, writing and spelling. Many children were inarticulate and many came from large families where they had only a small share of their mother's attention. There was a general lack of beauty about the environment which in the main consisted of slag heaps, bad housing and a small but heavily polluted river. The headmaster of the school, to use his own words, 'began as a boy in the days of chalk and talk, did much mechanical arithmetic, learned his grammar, history, geography and nature study from textbooks, and for most of the time had to be seen but not heard.'

But the school that the headmaster had created at Balby Street was different. The day started as a workshop. The children came early to prepare for their various activities, which generally began the day with arts and crafts. They helped each other and assumed an easy responsibility for the conditions in which they worked. The inside of the school was colourful and made impressive by its decoration, its displays of children's work, and its small exhibitions of things of beauty. As the headmaster put it at the time:

We start the day with what I would call a workshop atmosphere. The children come in before school and prepare for their various activities — painting, craft work and so on. This establishes a climate of purpose, but of course it is a burden on the teacher whose organization must be good. What we do at this time is establish social and indeed moral standards, as the children are all helping each other and assuming responsibility for the conditions in which they work, and for the groups with which they work. Incidentally it is worth noting that in these groups it is often the non-academic child who takes the lead.

When I visited the school a high proportion of the teachers were on probation or very young in their profession, and some were kind enough to write down the views which they formed when they first came to teach in the school. I have set out below the statements which they made.

The first teacher wrote:

I began work at Balby Street School in September 1972 with four years' training, three teaching practices and a Degree in Education, but, as I soon realized, I had very little preparation for the job I had to do. Looking back I can now see just how green I really was, and in many ways I suppose I still am.

I took far too many things for granted, expecting the children to have experience of far too many things. I am still surprised at times by their lack of vocabulary and experience. Last week even, I was talking about some moss feeling like velvet, when I noticed that some of the children were looking at me blankly: when I questioned them I found that some of them had never felt velvet and others knew the material but not its name. I was able to correct this because we had some velvet in the fabric box, but had this happened when I first started teaching, I would not have been sufficiently in tune with my class to notice that they were puzzled.

I had no idea then of the immense value of discussion. Oral work just never came into my scheme of things. I assumed that every lesson should have a tangible and usually written result. Now I find that we talk and talk and talk, sometimes writing about it afterwards, sometimes not.

Above all however, I had no idea of the immense value of praise. I thought it was something to be given out only for exceptional effort as a sort of prize. I have since realized of course that all children need praise for most of the things they do, provided they have tried hard. I did not realize that the work of poorer children must be compared with their previous work and any improvement recognized, even though a brighter child would be slated for the same piece of work. Similarly a bright child needs praise simply for keeping up a high standard without necessarily making a great stride each time. I think I had the idea that praise loses its value if it is used too much, but in practice this has proved quite false. Of course it must be justified, children soon realize if you are willing to accept low standards, and lose all respect for you if you do. As in everything else, it comes back to relationships. If you know a child well enough, you know what he is capable of, and how much encouragement he needs. At the same time if he respects you he will value your commendation and give his best to please you. A relationship like this is difficult for a beginner to develop at first, because you are unsure of yourself, and tend to concentrate on yourself rather than the children.

Mistakes like these are easy to analyse now, but at the time they are so difficult to see, largely because one is so involved with the job that it is difficult to stand back and view the situation objectively. In these circumstances a word of guidance from someone with experience can be invaluable. Again this reverts back to relationships, because advice must be both given and taken in the right spirit; and nobody resents criticism more than someone who feels he is failing.

At the same time, the work is so exhausting at first, and the sheer practical organization seems so complicated, that small problems soon get on top of you. When you cannot cope with everything at once, it is difficult without experience to get the priorities right. There is so much you need to learn for yourself, and your style of teaching must in the end be your own, but in the process both teacher and class seem to suffer.

It does not all come at once, and I suppose all teachers make mistakes, but once you realize where you are going and the children accept you, it is a marvellous feeling. Amongst all the harassment and nagging the simplest things bring home to you how important you are to some of your children, and how much you can give them. You see their wonder and excitement at the simplest things, such as looking through a microscope at a piece of moss. There are the sudden improvements in work which more than make up for all the weeks of plodding, which seemed to get nowhere. Particularly with the younger ones, it is grand to see them gaining confidence and independence as they realize their own worth and your appreciation of it. The boy who is slow in everything, but is interested in birds, will be proud when you ask his opinion on the subject, and at the same time, he will go up in the other children's estimation, and so much the better if it encourages him to read a bird book.

It is so rewarding when you find children staying behind at night to read, just so that they can take a new book home; or simply staying to help because they like being in school; even moaning on Friday because they cannot come on the next day to finish a piece of writing or a painting. Then you know that they really want to learn, and what more important feeling can you give them than this.

Your own self-esteem soars when you realize that children trust you, that they confide in you, knowing that you care. As in everything, the more you put in, the more you get out of teaching. The more you give children the more they give in return, in caring as well as academic work, and most of our children have so little, that it is so easy to give to them, and the rewards flow back.

The second teacher reported as follows:

When I received notification that I was to go to Balby Street Junior School, I knew a little about the area, as I had attended college in the area as a student. Also, I had a friend at college who was actually doing her final teaching practice at Balby Street. She was not having a very successful time, consequently she disliked it. When she heard that I was to go there, she advised me against it, painting a very gloomy picture of what I would face in the year to come. Therefore I first visited the school with very mixed feelings about what I should find. Later, at the end of her teaching practice, my friend envied my appointment.

I suppose one's teaching practice schools help to colour the imagination concerning the coming appointment. Mine had been dull disciplinary places where the teachers came into the staffroom at 8.50 a.m., sat drinking tea until the very last possible moment, then yawned, stretched and stated, 'Well, I wonder what I shall do with my lot today.' At the time it made me question what the profession is all about, now it makes me shudder. I remember going to Balby Street with the sole aim of becoming a better teacher than I had been a student.

When I finally came to see the school, I got off the bus at the bottom of the street and looked up to where the school stood, at the top of a steep climb. My home was situated in Surrey and I must confess I had never seen anything quite like that view before. As I walked up the road I peered in at the old houses and tried to imagine the children that lived in them — children I would probably be teaching.

But as I entered the school I was overwhelmed by the colour and liveliness that greeted me. The contrast between the drab atmosphere outside and the light and colour of the inside is something that will ever be imprinted on my mind. The staff themselves were smart in appearance and were all obviously very happy in their work.

The greatest difficulty I encountered once I got to school to begin my teaching career was coming to terms with certain facts. One fact was that although all the marvellous art and display work was around me, I was unable to achieve any of it. I was longing to be able to do the same but I had no experience whatsoever of this type of creativity. My headmaster constantly told me, when he knew of my worries, not to try to run before I could walk. The relationships teachers had, not only with the pupils in their charge but with all the pupils in the school, was something to be treasured, I felt. I had not got this kind of relationship. Consequently I lacked confidence. All this, I now realize, cannot be achieved in five minutes. It takes time, effort and a great deal of caring. But once I became a part of the school, and got to know the routines and standards, I felt I could make a success of my appointment. I then had to prove to others that I could.

I am now in my third year of teaching and am at a stage where I am at last ready and able to start 'running'. I feel an able part of the teaching staff, and have got over many of the teething troubles which face a young teacher, but I realize that I still have a great wealth of knowledge and experience to gather. During the last year I have taken over and added to the guitar group, a major part of my life at Balby Street. This challenge has been an enormous confidence builder. The task seemed awesome at first, but with the encouragement and support of the headmaster and senior staff, I feel I have been able to bring a degree of success to it.

My greatest salvation during the early days at Balby Street was the tremendous help and enthusiasm given to me by more experienced members of the staff. We work as a team, sharing each other's ideas, successes and troubled moments. I, myself, am enjoying every minute of school. I cannot get there fast enough in the morning — not to sit with a cup of tea, but to get into my room to make sure it is ready for when the first of my charges arrive. I find plenty to do at lunch time, either guitar practices or work in the classroom. Often, I like to stay at school for an extra hour or so to work on a new display, or change the art work around. Enthusiastic readers in my class love to read to me after school. I often say at the end of the day, 'those wishing to stay and read, remain sitting,' easily half always remain sitting.

My headmaster has always called my classroom my shop window. It reflects me and my attitude. I want my room to be a lovely place to be in, I want my children to be pleasant children to be with. My class and I work at this together. Gradually we are building an understanding of each other. We care for each other and for the room we spend so much time together in. I now feel I have a special relationship with my class just budding. A few days ago, the new 'floating' teacher and I took my class down the road to watch some of the now empty houses being knocked down. Neil, being very excited watching the bulldozer eating its way through the brickwork, ran to us, looked up at the other teacher about to enthuse about what he had seen, then stopped, turned to me, gave me a big smile and burst forth with what he had to say. That, for me, has been a turning point in all I have worked to build up this term. I matter to those children, and they matter to me. I can go home satisfied at the end of my day, because I know I have put everything I have into it. I have given those children part of me, and their response means everything.

The third teacher wrote:

With only a limited contact with schools behind me (three teaching practices of one month each over three years) my experience of the day-to-day running of a school was restricted, as is the case with most students. During these practices, I had not been in contact with the kind of involvement in teaching that I have now experienced. The teachers I observed had a routine attitude towards teaching, and I think I rather expected this to be the case once my college course was over. Had it not been for the headmaster at Balby Street, I think I would have fitted into a routine, rather than experiencing, as I do now, the excitement that some situations can bring. When I was embarking on my teaching, I was very aware of the responsibility of guiding the education of thirty or so children for a full year. What I did, my attitudes and values, would have an effect on these children.

I knew a little about Balby Street before I actually started teaching. I had visited one evening after school, and had felt the impact of colour and life after the somewhat forbidding exterior. I realized then the challenge which faced me, and was rather apprehensive about my ability to cope. After my appointment to the school, I spent a few days in classrooms, and was impressed by the range of activities and experiences I was expected to provide. Once again I questioned my own resourcefulness. I also spent a week in the Infant Department, getting to know the children who would become my first year junior class in the following September, so that at least I knew a little about them. During the summer holiday, before I began my probationary year, I spent a couple of days in my future classroom, familiarizing myself with its equipment and books. I did not, therefore, begin my probationary year without some groundwork.

Even so, when I started teaching, I was really aware of how unprepared I was. I could see the rooms of the other teachers and their confidence with display work and I, myself, felt completely unable to organize my room satisfactorily. I felt it was important that the room should be well organized to promote a good working attitude, and I wanted it to look interesting and exciting so that the children would enjoy working in it. Although I had lots of opportunities to look at other rooms, I think it is only by struggling with the problem that a solution can be achieved. After many different attempts and experiments, I managed to get the kind of organization which suited my particular needs.

I think the major problem I had to face as a probationary teacher was to achieve in my own classroom the standards of work I could see in other people's rooms around the school. It is only when the teacher knows the children that she can get the best from them. It also means that she, the teacher herself, must have an awareness of quality before the children gain it too. The teacher has to be aware of beauty before she can help the children to see it, and she has constantly to adapt and develop to new situations.

The satisfactions of teaching at Balby Street are enormous, and yet I find it extremely difficult to say exactly what they are. I think it is important for teachers as well as for children, to work in a happy, calm atmosphere. New personal confidence is gained when successes in the classroom give a greater incentive to go further, and also compensate to some extent for failures. What the children achieve in the classroom, is a little part of me, and I feel I have played a small part in the development of their attitudes and skills. The 'class feeling', when everyone works hard and does their best in an atmosphere of trust, is the great strength of Balby Street, and it is this which gives the greatest satisfaction.

One of the most significant features of these three statements is that relatively little is said in them about the teacher's technical task of transmitting knowledge to her pupils. Great attention, however, is paid to such matters as colour and display inside the schools, to the importance of enjoyment in learning, and to other sensitive efforts which aim at creating sound and happy relationships between teacher and child.

It is emphases such as these which raise serious doubts about our more traditional ways of training teachers. Unfortunately it is much easier in the training process to pass on the textbook pedagogy than it is to nurture the attitudes to learning which result in caring, concern and enjoyment.

There is an obvious case for enabling a teacher in training to continue his advanced studies for the first two years at college or university, but it might be much better if thereafter the student were to spend a full year in the schools, and then finish his course with a year of theory. If this were done, the student would gain much in maturity of experience before concluding his course, and certainly his training college lecturers would have to keep their minds very much refreshed and alive if they had to handle students who came to them from a year's experience in the classroom.

Studies in the theory of teaching can give the intending teacher a basis from which he learns, but it is work in the schools which introduces him to the practicalities, and to the more spiritual essence of his task. The ability to teach really well is something that one is born with or something which is caught from gifted colleagues; it can rarely be implanted or taken from the textbook.

10

Parents

The anxieties of parents about the primary school that their children will attend are revealed by the kind of questions that they ask. 'Do they get them on?' 'Do they let them run wild?' 'Do they teach them manners?' 'My child's not very bright, will she be passed over?' 'Do they lark about in the toilets?' 'Do they cane them?' 'How many get into trouble with the police?' 'Do they let them do as they like?' 'I was good at games. Do they look after that side?' . . and so on. Questions such as these reveal that most parents know what they want from the primary school to which they send their children, and in the vast majority of cases their wants are legitimate, valid and eminently sensible. Their children, they say, should learn to read and write and do arithmetic, so that they can manage their affairs and do well in the secondary school, and get a job when they leave it. Some believe that their children should also know something of the Bible, and do a little drawing and painting and music. They should learn to speak clearly and behave properly amongst themselves and with others.

All parents have themselves been to school, and they remember something of what happened to them while they were there. If they are normal, contented and successful people, they will tend to be in favour of the same things being done to their children as were done with them. Most were, for instance, taught mechanically to add and subtract, to multiply and divide, and to 'do problems'; even if they disliked all this, as many did, they believe that their children should go through the same routines. They recall how their teacher wrote important words on the blackboard, so that these could be used in composition, and they expect their children to have the same sort of experience. The day should begin with assembly, and then with arithmetic, 'while the children are fresh', for this is what they did. Spelling lists must be learned, and they suppose that children must still be made to practise intelligence tests, even if they no longer have to take the dreaded 11 plus. There will be daily mental arithmetic, but also some time to make things, as part of the craft lessons, and there will be some physical education and games, and sometimes visits out of school.

And of course most parents believe that the attitudes of their day should still apply, at least to some extent. By and large, children should be seen and not heard, they should 'know their place', they should be aware of the rules, and should obey them. Naturally they will be taught in class groups, the clever ones together, the middling ones together and the dull ones together. Competition will be important, 'it makes the children work,' marks will be the main reward and punishment, corporal punishment if necessary will be the main deterrent. Many of the schools which worked in this way and held these beliefs, were happy and effective places, and it is their pupils who have created, and still are creating, the world as we know it.

But parents have two main worries. They know that there are good schools and bad schools and that wherever there are several schools one will be the worst. They know that schools and teaching methods have changed somewhat, but they do not know quite how, nor whether the changes are for the better. However most parents are now much more aware of their rights in these matters than they used to be. They are represented on governing and managing bodies, and they are better prepared and more ready to press authorities on such personal matters as the choice of school for their children. The more knowledgeable of them are aware that by law, although it is the parents' responsibility to have their children educated, the authorities must offer such choice of school 'as is compatible with the provision of efficient instruction and the avoidance of unreasonable expenditure'.

When discussing these matters, it is normal to make the assumption that all children are reared in normally acceptable conditions, that is to say, that they will enjoy reasonable warmth and food and clothing, that not more than six people will share two bedrooms, that each home will have an indoor toilet and fixed bath, and at least a dozen books. But this is a generalization which heads of schools in many areas could not possibly assume. In the worst areas there are schools which claim that a quarter to a third of their children lack at least two of these amenities, though at the other more comfortable extreme there are heads who will rightly affirm that few of their pupils lack any.

Schools have always to bear in mind the fact that it is the parents and the homes which so often make children happy or unhappy, and as Bertrand Russell put it, 'Children are good because they are happy, and not happy because they are good.' There is also no doubt whatever that the expectations of a home, as well as its happiness, have a powerful effect on the education of its children.

Parents divide themselves into a variety of categories. There are those who themselves have been right through the educational system and know the educational ropes. The thought never enters their heads that their children will do other than they did, namely go through the school system to college or university, and this expectation is lodged with their children from their earliest years, and becomes a powerful force in their attitude to learning.

There are parents who themselves failed to follow this course, and are powerfully anxious that no child of theirs should suffer a similar failure. They are determined to succeed through their children, and their ambition, at best, gives their children powerful support, and at worst, creates in them a distaste for all the learning that they are forced to do.

Then of course there are the parents who are school shy. They disliked school, and were its failures. They do not want to be reminded of their failure, and they find it difficult to respond to any overtures which the school might wish to make in connection with their children's upbringing.

None of these categories of parents need necessarily damage their children, but all can contain sub-categories which produce our most serious problem children. There are parents who are utter failures as such, and who, at worst, hate their children. There are parents who so hate each other that they fight and quarrel or vie one with the other for their child's affection, or parents who spoil their children, or ignore and resent them. Then of course, there are children with sick, maimed, or elderly parents, parents who may be admirable and loving, but whose defects create severe family problems, and increasingly there are immigrant parents to many of whom school is an unknown quantity with aspirations alien to their own.

Most schools can produce illustrations of the damage that the worst parents can inflict on their children. The following are fairly typical examples taken from a school community centre in a reasonably problem-free area of a small town during one half day's visit.

(a) A fifteen-year-old told his teacher of the bitter relationship which had developed with his mother because she believed that he was having a homosexual relationship with a company director. The father frequently assaulted his wife and children and from time to time locked them out of the house.

(b) A woman lived with her husband, and in the same building cohabited with other men, one of whom from time to time battered her and the children. One of her four children, a boy of eight, had fits of violence and threw objects round the room. At school he had violent tantrums in which he beat and kicked other children, and tried to do the same to his teacher.

(c) A mother and father utterly neglected their six children, three of whom fell into the hands of the police. The mother eventually left home with another man and the father avoided and completely neglected his own offspring. One of the children, who has now been taken into care, knew himself to be too dirty to attend school. He was given no dinner money, was poorly fed at home and, when his mother left the family, his father made him sleep in the coal shed at night.

(d) In one family of twelve, the father had been out of work for years, and relied on threats to maintain order in the home. One of his children was so grossly unkempt and ill clad that she cried about it desperately at school. Eventually the staff acquired clothes into which the child changed on arrival at school, where she was also washed or bathed.

(e) One father had long bouts of heavy drinking after which from time to time he smashed up the furniture of the home. He had twice tried to set the house on fire. His wife, from whom he was divorced, still lived with him in the same house, and the children frequently had to witness their mother being beaten up by their father. There were six children, one a spastic and one in borstal. A third child was timid and shy and jealous of his spastic brother. His outlet was in temper tantrums, in one of which he attacked his sister with a scythe. He had no friends.

A Community School for girls can produce equally severe cases.

(f) A mother, having had a number of children by unknown men, eventually married a youth of eighteen.

(g) A girl ran away from home, and her mother later did likewise. The girl came back home to her father and was subject to incest.

(h) In one family the step-father had not spoken to a child for two years. The mother was allowed to go out with the man's children, but the girl to whom he would not speak was not allowed to go with her own mother.

(i) In one home a crazed mother insisted on putting on gloves and wiping the seat every time her daughter used the toilet.

(j) In a family with two black parents, the father died and the mother married an elderly white man. Then the mother died and the black children were left to the care of the elderly white man, who had no affection for them.

One runs several dangers in compiling lists of this kind. The first is that one sees only the bad, and forgets that most children have a happy home; and many from unhappy homes are so tough and resilient that they survive and become normal and healthy adults. But a still greater danger is that we forget that these children do exist, and even if there is only one per school, this will make a total of several hundreds in each of the larger local authorities.

A third point is that the list I have quoted was compiled by me after two brief visits to two schools only, and that a thorough search in the areas concerned would reveal many more cases, all of them severe and deeply disturbing. Furthermore, we must always remember that the cases quoted are merely those that come to light, and that in every school and every Authority, the children as a whole could be graduated from those who suffer intolerable misery, to those whose happiness in life gives them every chance; and that a child who lacks resilience may succumb to pressures which are far lighter than those illustrated by the cases I have quoted.

There are, I suspect, a variety of categories of children who suffer in these ways. For instance, I recently had the privilege of reading some very fine writing by a number of adolescents in a Community Home School for disruptive girls, girls whose behaviour is such that they are no longer allowed in normal society. But the quality of the writing revealed an unquestioned sensitivity, and one is driven to conclude that it is this sensitivity which is characteristic of their normal personality, and that they have been driven to coarseness and repulsive behaviour as a kind of defence, which enables them to stand up to the dreadful circumstances into which they have all too often been born and have had to live.

There are reasons for disruptive behaviour to which we have given too little attention but which could to some extent explain our current wave of violence and hooliganism. The parents of our older trouble-making teenagers were themselves very small when family life was disturbed by the worst years of depression in the early thirties. The parents of our younger teenagers were denied a completely satisfying family life by evacuation. Thus it is that two groups of parents were themselves denied the experience of a sound, healthy and enjoyable upbringing, and cannot therefore pass on these qualities to their own children.

It is difficult for an observer in these matters, as distinct from a practitioner, to say what ought to be done to help parents who for one reason or another are failing. But we know of at least some of the attempts that are being made. We all know of the need to include parents on governing bodies, and to encourage active parent-teacher associations. Many schools now use volunteer parents as 'extra pairs of ears' for children to read to, and extra adults for them to talk with. Some schools are now using liaison-teachers to help in those homes which may be excellent at keeping their children fit and co-operative, but are unsure about taking the first educational steps in the home.

Parents are more and more being brought into school to take part in normal or special assemblies, in ways which will enable them to see what changes are taking place, and how the home can help. The help that is being given by parents is not confined to help by mothers. I so well remember the shock I had when I arrived at a primary school to find the playground being torn up systematically by a team of expert fathers who were about to connect to the mains a heated swimming pool that they had just constructed. There are varieties of ways used by schools to keep parents informed of what is happening in the classrooms and of course schools are more and more being used by communities out of school hours. It is above all important that schools should make welcoming contacts with parents before the child begins his school career and that this contact should form the basis of future close collaboration between the two bodies, the home and the school, which will be responsible for the child's growth and development.

The more the school can ensure this continued contact by

meetings with individual parents, meetings with parents' associations, statements to parents as to how the school hopes to work, reports, verbal and written, to the parents whose children need special help, the greater will be the confidence and competence with which the parents will support the school's aims and endeavours.

It is of vital importance that the best practice of this kind should be made known amongst the schools of an area. Every local education authority in the country has a handful of schools which are more effective than others in what they do to enlist parental help, and how they use it, and their success should be made known to others, preferably by small discussion groups or by visits of individual teachers to successful schools, particularly if what has to be conveyed is the atmosphere and attitude in which collaboration is taking place.

11

Caretakers

There are a number of important tasks outside the curriculum which can greatly enhance or damage the quality of a school. There is, for instance, the whole of the school meals service, and the work of school secretaries, of welfare officers and of caretakers. Of these and other ancillary services the only one which I dealt with at first hand was the caretaking service, and it is for this reason that I wish to make a few points about it which I believe to be of importance.

What is its real significance? Edward Thring made this statement about his work as a headmaster, and in it he sets the background to my own views about the need to care for the school building:

God did not think it beneath His Majesty to give special orders, during the time He was training and educating His people, as to the material and making of robes, the colour of ribands, the artistic disposition of a fringe, and I unhesitatingly assert that my own work has succeeded with the many, just because God gave me a spirit of wisdom to attend to fringes, and blue and purple and scarlet ribands, and Pompeian red, and autotypes, and boys' studies and the colour of curtains to their compartments and a number of little things of this kind. And I lay claim to having been great as a schoolmaster on this, and on this only in the main, on having had the sense to work with tools, to follow God's guidance in teaching beginners, by surrounding them as He did with noble and worthy surroundings, taking care that there was no meanness or neglect; getting rid as circumstances allowed of all the little vilenesses which drag the boy-mind down. It is a slow process but a true one, it is not grand, but it is practical, it needs patience but it works by degrees to higher life. . . I take my stand on detail.

Local authorities are required by law to contribute to the spiritual, moral, mental and physical well-being of the community, and in that order. We do not always realize how powerfully the surroundings into which we put children can influence these aims.

At the outbreak of the last war, buildings were being requisitioned and earmarked for military and civil defence purposes, and Mrs Mee, HMI, and a local man with authority to requisition were looking at likely buildings in a black-country town. They came upon a small dismal school on an island site and the man put his head inside the school porch and in all seriousness said, 'Ah yes, this will do for the mortuary,' and moved on to the next building.

In those days it was still possible to find hanging on the wall of a school the 'Monarch of the Glen' in sepia, prints of Edward VII and Queen Alexandra, and diagrams of the human skeleton or the bloodstream, and when a child asked to 'leave the room' he had in some schools to tear a piece of paper from the roll hanging obscenely on a piece of string near the blackboard. I well remember seeing one roll hung immediately on the left of the entrance of a large modern school. Changing the attitude which could permit such practices and helping teachers and caretakers to convert schools into places of aesthetic delight was one of the most rewarding tasks in which I have ever taken part. I realized its significance early in life.

The County Secondary School at Long Eaton in Derbyshire where my father was the first headmaster set my standards. Its corridors and classrooms were panelled, and above the panelling in each classroom were beautifully painted friezes of the Chaucer Tales. There was also a Milton room, a French room, a room with paintings of local lace factories. Copies of famous works of art in facsimile frames made in the school woodwork room were hung in the corridors and classrooms and show cases in the hall were used for the display of Greek coins and Japanese netsukes, and other small articles of beauty.

The two caretakers, whom I still remember so well, kept the school spotless, and I never recall any abuse of the school walls by the pupils. As head of the school my father used almost daily to pay a brief visit to the toilets and other remote parts of the building to see that all was clean and decent. It was, I think, as early as this that I began to realize that the caretaker's job is more than merely cleaning the school and making it an attractive place in which instruction can be given. What he can in effect do is enhance the quality of the environment in such a way that it makes a subtle but powerful contribution to the education which the school provides.

This view was vastly strengthened when I went to the West Riding. The war had just ended, many schools had inevitably been neglected for years, and many were in such a lamentable condition that I felt it essential to share the responsibility by reporting on what I had seen very fully to the Committee and its Chairman. There were about 3000 caretakers and cleaners working in some 1200 schools, and much that was done in the name of cleaning was bad. Floors were swilled, paste polish was applied by cleaners on their knees, and there was much in the schools' ways which created dirt and dust. The Committee appointed Ernest Peet as their Supervisor of Caretakers. He was himself a distinguished and experienced caretaker who had no difficulty in working easily and in full agreement with the team of architects and art advisers and others who were called upon to bring about a revolution in school decoration and maintenance. Methods of cleaning were changed, emphasis was put on prevention as it was realized that an hour spent on keeping dirt out of a school saved many hours removing it once it was in.

Door mats were introduced of a size which meant that a child had to take several steps in order to cross them; and samples of every type of floor were converted into test panels which were used in order to find out by experience the best ways of maintaining them. New tools were devised, new techniques developed and new colour schemes evolved, but most important of all was the care that was given to the caretakers themselves.

Residential courses for caretakers were conducted at Woolley Hall, the centre for the in-service training of teachers which was opened in 1952. Each course covered three days, and fees and travelling expenses were paid by the Authority. The arrangements were in the hands of Ernest Peet, who would invite me as Chief Education Officer and our Art Adviser, Basil Rocke, to make our contribution. Basil Rocke's job was to talk with teachers, architects and caretakers about colour-schemes for the schools, and he would invariably display pictures in order to emphasize the care that they needed to take if they were to bring about the interest and delight which was their purpose.

My task was to emphasize the importance of the caretaker's work as an educating force, and I felt it to be of special importance. Sometimes, as a result of pressure of work, I had to decline an invitation to take part in a teachers' course, but I do not think that I ever refused to open one of the caretakers' courses once I was asked to do so. On these courses, scale plans and models of schools were used to promote sound organization; film slides and other visual aids were used to illustrate standards; and the caretakers themselves took an ever-increasing share of the work as instructors. The boiler house at Woolley Hall, in addition to heating the building, became a demonstration centre which showed how such a place should be used and tended. A handbook entitled *A New Approach to Clean Schools* raised standards in the county and was in demand by the thousand not only in this country but as far afield as Canada and the USA.

So successful were the developments that the Authority decided to establish a permanent centre at Woolley Hall where training on a much larger scale could proceed throughout the year. This centre was opened in 1969. It comprises an exhibition area, lecture rooms, workshops and stores. In addition to its permanent exhibition of standard equipment, there was a changing display of items designed to meet special needs, and the items exhibited varied from a tap washer to a time switch, from an ash tray to a bulk waste container, from a nail brush to an electric scrubber.

Courses were provided throughout the year, not only for those who worked in schools, but for workers from other County Council establishments and departments. There were also courses for newly-appointed caretakers and specialist courses which dealt with such matters as floor maintenance, the care of carpets and fabrics, the operation of heating installations and so on. But it is probably true to say that the most valuable outcome of what has been done at Woolley Hall has been the sharing of the responsibility of school maintenance between teachers, caretakers and cleaners. The centre has been much visited by teachers from home and abroad, and it is now not unusual for a head teachers' course to include a session on caretaking, or for teachers and advisers to play their part in caretakers' courses.

There is one important point which should be made, as it affects caretaking. It is difficult to write off used stock which teachers have a propensity for storing. The consequence is that schools manage to collect massive piles of what, in the light of their current methods, can only be described as 'junk'. I once organized a 'throw out your dead' campaign in the County, and the County Supplies Department collected eight van loads of unwanted and unusable material from the first six schools they visited! I would not for one moment assert that a clean and well-cared-for school is inevitably a good school, but I have known very few good schools which are dirty and ill-cared-for. To any one who knows and visits schools, it is blatantly obvious that an ill-cared-for school creates wrong attitudes and invites wrong behaviour. A panel or piece of wall that is broken and needs repair will, unless it is quickly treated, be further damaged; if pupils' work is ill-displayed, the youngsters will rightly deduce the teacher's lack of concern; if notice boards are untidy, the message they convey will be less significant; if the teachers' appearance is unkempt, or their staffrooms are squalid, the children's standards will be lowered accordingly; if pictures are allowed to stay hung until they fade, the children will hold them to be of no account; and when all these things happen, it is almost inevitable that the child's spiritual and moral well-being will suffer; and of course the caretaker's job will then be made infinitely more difficult.

I cannot over-emphasize the need for a right relationship between the caretaking and teaching staff. Both are concerned with the welfare and growth, physical and spiritual, of the children in the school. Edward Thring was clear about this, as my opening quotation to this chapter revealed. The following statement from his book also leaves no doubt about his views.

Another grave cause of evil is the dishonour shown to the place in which the work is done. Things are allowed to be left about and not put away when finished with; great roughness is permitted in the treatment of the room and its furniture. Yet there is no law more absolutely certain than that mean treatment produces mean ideas.

12

Inspectors, Advisers and Administrators

It was in 1833 that Parliament first voted money, a sum of £20,000, to assist voluntary efforts to educate the children of the labouring poor. The way this money was used was at first not subject to inspection, but six years later, when an education committee of the Privy Council was established, it was decided that no future grants should be made unless the Queen had the right to send her inspectors to the school which was being helped, to find out whether the grant was being wisely used. The man in charge of the Privy Council's Committee on Education was Dr Kay, the assistant Poor Law Commissioner, and he appointed the first Inspectors and issued these instructions, amongst others, to them:

It is of the utmost consequence that you should bear in mind that this inspection is not intended as a means of exercising control, but of affording assistance; that it is not to be regarded as operating for the restraint of local efforts, but for their encouragement and that its chief objects will not be attained without the co-operation of the school committees; the inspector having no power to interfere and being instructed not to offer any advice or information excepting where it is invited.

The main points of these early instructions were that the Inspectors should assist teachers and managers to achieve better things, and that the school should become the centre of community life. The attention of the Inspectors was also drawn to matters which are still the subject of our vital concern such as the provision of playgrounds, relations between parents and teachers, the maintenance of the interest of former scholars and the provision and accessibility of a school library. The impression given by some of these early instructions is one of wisdom, vision and enlightenment.

Unfortunately Dr Kay Shuttleworth, as he had become, had to retire in 1849 because of ill health, and much of his wisdom was lost. His successor was Robert Lowe who believed in all that Kay had rejected, and, following the report of a national commission in 1861, he decided that teachers should be paid according to the results which their pupils obtained when tested by HMI. Lowe's complaint was that the schools were too much concerned with the 'impalpable essences' of education, and he introduced the 'Code' or common core of those days, to effect a change from the 'hyacinths' to the 'loaves'. This Code set out precisely what schools in receipt of government grants had to teach, and how they had to teach it. Kay Shuttleworth condemned it for the mechanical drudgery which it imposed on child, teacher and HMI, and Matthew Arnold, himself an Inspector, said of it, 'It makes the action of the state upon popular education as mechanical as possible and in the game of mechanical contrivances, the teacher will, in the end, always defeat us.' Thus it was that even when the service started, there existed this antithesis between mind and spirit, to which I have already referred. It is a permanent antithesis, and though all Inspectors and Advisers are aware of both sides, some will lean to the mental and measurable while others are constantly aware of the need to nourish the growth of the spirit.

The question is often asked, 'Why should we have to have Inspectors and Advisers?' and I have no doubt whatever about the need. It has always been there and always will be. To express this need at its lowest level one has to point out that there will always be at any given moment one Authority which is the worst in the country, and the Government which distributes the tax-payers' money must be in a position to take action against such an Authority once it knows that public money is being ill spent. I well recall an occasion when year after year one of Her Majesty's Inspectors, whom I knew very well, refused to sign the official form stating that a certain major Authority was spending its money according to the rules. Eventually the Ministry of Education, as it then was, had to take full note of the situation and force the offending Authority to mend its ways by withholding its grant. There are many other situations which call for what used to be known as a full inspection. If an Authority has doubts about a school, it may wish to have an opinion other than, or in addition to, that provided by its own advisory staff. There may be circumstances in which a head and his school are subjected to gross local criticism and here again there may be a need for an expert outside opinion. A head may take over a very difficult school, and it may be in the interests of all concerned to secure a report by HMI on the school as soon as the new head takes over.

But it would be quite wrong to assume that the job of HMI is solely to find out what is wrong and tell the LEA to put it right. All schools need recognition and support and the central government which provides much of the money needs to know of the difficulties which different Authorities have to face. It is for reasons such as these that there should be visiting our schools a select and largely independent body of men and women who not only possess the sympathy, humility (and I stress this word) and the enthusiasm which are the essential characteristics of any first-rate teacher, but who also have acquired by experience and training personal attitudes which will command respect and will inspire and encourage. This matter of personality in one who visits schools to offer help is of the utmost importance, for if he lacks experience he will not carry conviction, if he lacks humility, he will fail to support, if he is tedious he will fail to inspire and if he lacks courage his independence will falter. It is the independence of the HMI and his experience of a number of Authorities that makes his judgement so valuable.

The Local Authority Adviser is in a somewhat different position. He too will diagnose and report, but he will also have the task of effecting a cure, not only of the faults which he has found, but of those revealed by HMI. This he may do by more frequent visits to the school than the HMI with his wider area can manage. He may call upon colleagues who are subject specialists to visit the school, he may ask an advisory teacher to help the school, or he may recommend certain teachers on the staff of the criticized school to undertake courses in those areas of the curriculum where weaknesses have been disclosed. Thus the straightforward task of the Adviser is to strengthen the weak teacher with encouragement and helpful suggestions, including the teacher's attendance at courses and visits to other schools. If the art or housecraft or music is weak, Advisers with a specialist background will be asked to offer help; if the general subjects are faulty, an Adviser with experience in this field will be called in.

There are a few Advisers who have the supreme gift of being able, by wisdom, kindness and encouragement, to transform a school, and in some who are able to do this there is an element of genius. I well remember a colleague of mine who had this particular gift. If he found a school which was slack he could be very firm and direct; if, however, he found one that was doing a poor best, he would apply a more sensitive cure. He would look around the school until he found something he could commend. He would then say to the teacher, John Smith, 'I wish there were more work of this quality,' and in a few weeks' time, when he went again to the school, there would be more of the work, and John Smith would have given some thought as to why his work was judged to be good. On the second visit the Adviser would rejoice in the work that had been done and would take the school head to John Smith's room in order to spread the conception of quality. By this time both John Smith and his headmaster would not only be aware that the work was good but they would have thought about it educationally, and would know why it was good. At his next visit to the school, the Adviser might ask John Smith to come along one evening to talk to teachers of a neighbouring school who were operating in a similar way, and by this time John Smith would be excited about what he was doing with such success. Finally Smith would be asked to talk to a teacher's course about his work, and the thought and perception engendered by this daunting experience would have made a notable difference to his potential as a teacher.

The organization of an Authority's advisory staff is important. There are, as I have already said, three tasks to be performed; one is to see that standards are high and subjects well taught, the second is to ensure that the school has all that it needs, and the third is to give support and recognition. An effective way of doing this is to see that each member of the advisory team has a dual role. He will, in his first role, advise on the teaching of this or that subject, and the schools for which he is responsible may be distributed over a wide area. But he may also be given a pastoral task in relation to a small group of schools in a much smaller area. His tasks with these schools will be to make sure that each school has what it needs by way of material provision, and also to act as the school's friend, to offer it recognition, support and encouragement.

Dangers can arise out of a system of inspection, and these have been fully documented in the past. In the early days of the 'Code' or 'Common Core' as we might name it the central administration used the Inspectorate to enforce practices to which some of the Inspectors themselves were hostile. HMI Matthew Arnold held that the Code so narrowed the work of the Inspector that it was 'as if the generals of an army were to have their duties limited to inspecting the men's cartouche boxes'. He said that the Code had been concocted in the recesses of the Privy Council Office with no advice asked of those practically conversant with the schools, and no notice given to those who supported the schools. In the House, Lord Robert Cecil moved a resolution to the effect that:

In the opinion of this House, the mutilation of the reports of Her

Majesty's Inspectors of Schools and the exclusion from them of statements and opinions adverse to the educational views entertained by the Committee of Council, while matter favourable to them is admitted, are variations of the understanding under which the appointment of inspectors was originally sanctioned by Parliament, and tend entirely to destroy the value of the reports.

There are other ways in which the system can go wrong. The advisory staff may be called upon to do far too much paper work, and, what is even worse, they may see their increase in paper work as something which enhances their status. An individual Inspector or Adviser may lose all humility and exert a damaging authority on the schools he visits. He may take too active a part in the promotion of staff. On this matter I have seen two extremes. In Australia, with its vast territories, it is often the local Inspector who is responsible for promotions, and what he does and says can carry far too much weight. At the other extreme, I recall an occasion when the advisory staff of the West Riding asked to be freed from playing any part in staff promotions as the knowledge that they did so spoiled their relationships with the heads and staffs in the schools that they served.

There is one danger which I have found to prevail amongst less thoughtful Advisers. I see no reason why an Adviser should not distribute information about the methods and techniques of teaching reading or arithmetic or history or any other factual subject. When it comes to the more aesthetic activities: art, the crafts, dance and so on, it is a different matter. The purpose of these activities is not to discover and promote professional artists but to stimulate ways of expression which will develop the child's own individuality and sensitivity. The danger occurs when the teacher or Adviser, having studied a particular skill himself to an advanced level, imposes that technique on young pupils and so thwarts their personal expressive development. This is a particular danger in young adults who hoped to become performers but who have had to fall back, as they see it, on teaching and who try to gain satisfaction by making their pupils do what they through inability failed to do.

Any statement on inspection and advice should in my view conclude with the warning that the person who is responsible for what happens in a classroom is in the eyes of the Authority not the Inspector, or the Adviser, but the teacher. This point of view was put very cogently by Sir Percival Sharpe, when he was the Director of Education for Sheffield. He sent out the following letter to the heads of the schools in the City:

Dear Sir (Madam)

Arising out of the consideration by the Education Committee of a report of the Board of Education on a school under the direction of the Education Committee, I desire to make clear to Head Teachers the fact that they are responsible to the Education Committee and to that Committee only, for the work, conduct and organization of their schools and to remind them that, while it is the function of the officers of the Board of Education and of the Committee's own Inspectors of Schools to make constructive suggestions by formal Report or otherwise for the consideration of Head Teachers, the responsibility for accepting or rejecting such suggestions must remain with the Head Teachers themselves. Further that no instructions of any kind may be issued to Head Teachers except by or on behalf of the Education Committee or the Managers of a School through the Committee's Executive Officer, or through the corresponding Manager of the School.

It is understood that during visits to schools it is not at all an unusual procedure on the part of the Board's Officers and of the Committee's Inspectors to make suggestions which, in their opinion, would be conducive to the betterment of the work, conduct and organization of the School. For the most part, these suggestions are based upon knowledge and experience and as such are worthy of and should receive the most careful consideration. Notwithstanding this, it is expected that Head Teachers will not adopt suggestions about which they have substantial doubts as to their wisdom or practicability merely on the grounds of amiable or even of courteous acquiescence. The responsibility for the efficiency or inefficiency of a school must in all cases and circumstances remain with the Head Teacher.

The only limitations placed upon a Head Teacher's responsibility are those which are inherent in instructions given to him as indicated above.

Having quoted this historical warning, I must admit that I have no doubt about the value of a good HMI. He can give encouragement and support of a kind which will stimulate and at best inspire a school. And when the worst comes to the worst, he can approach the Authority, and if his fears are confirmed he can ensure that the matters of which he is critical are put right.

But it is possible for the powers of the HMIs to become too great. They can become the tool of a central government which seeks to encroach on the powers of the local authority or of individual schools. They can be used to propagate a government doctrine which may appear to be in the national interest but which may have little to do with getting the best out of every child. When the force of HMIs was first established, Kay Shuttleworth inspired them with the highest ideals and did all in his power to sustain their independence and make sure that they did not become the slaves of government; by and large this tradition has been maintained and it is much to be hoped that it will continue.

The Local Authority Adviser employed by a bad Authority is subject to the same kind of pressures from his employing committee as those which are brought to bear on HMI by an unwise or ill-inclined central government; but he is subject to other dangers. At best he will be able to inspire and encourage as does HMI, but at worst he may bring a malign influence to bear on the way funds are spent and he may also, by the in-service training facilities which are at his disposal, propagate wrong and even dangerous doctrines.

Having uttered these warnings it would be wrong if I did not state that they apply with equal force to the administrative staff of an Authority. Indeed in some, if not in most, Authorities educational quality is determined by the attitudes which build up between the teachers on the one hand and the administration as represented by the central office staff on the other.

It is a relatively easy matter for the senior officers of an Authority to devise smooth running office machinery to ensure that their schools are well built, kept in good repair and well staffed, but the force which produces educational achievement of a high order will depend on the encouragement and recognition which the office staff and the schools give to each other.

The major task of a chief officer who is deeply concerned with the quality of his schools is to encourage and support those of his outside staff who can detect good practice and make real endeavours to see that such practice spreads throughout the service. The job of the central office of any Authority is to give the right support to the school at the right time and in the right amount, and to do this there must be adequate delegation.

The overwhelming developments of the early post-war years forced chief officers not only to delegate, but also to learn from teachers, Advisers and administrative colleagues who were all experimenting with new ways. I found myself developing a powerful interest in new junior-school discoveries and in the birth of comprehensive schools at the secondary stage. We recast our administration into divisional areas, we examined differently in that we attached more importance to teachers' opinions, we developed resource centres, music centres, adventure training centres, in-service training centres, and world famous figures such as Kurt Hahn, Laban, Cizek, and Herbert Read influenced what we did. In this period of almost frantic development I should have been disastrously submerged had I not been able to delegate to people who in their own specialities knew far more than I did.

But at this time I was most fortunate in many of my most experienced colleagues. Our Senior Inspector at this time, Miss V. E. C. Gordon, was a woman who had had very considerable experience as the head of a modern school, and educationally she was as wise and gifted as anyone with whom I have ever worked. Furthermore I had as my deputy Jim Hogan, who had established the first Outward Bound school and, working with Reg Eyles our post-school Adviser, he recast the whole of the West Riding further education service into a cohesive area organization. Equally important, however, was the support that he gave to John Gavall, our brilliant guitar playing music Adviser, in establishing music centres and orchestras all over the county. While doing this he completely reformed my attitude to and concern for voluntary organizations.

Most of our Advisers came to us already rich in classroom experience, but the best of them grew vastly in wisdom as they worked with the best of our teachers. A team of Advisers and administrators working in this way develops a spiritual zest which is catching and which at its best can stimulate the whole service, its schools, its colleges and even its committees. This is something which happens as a result of the attitudes which are engendered; it cannot be contrived.

13

Councillors

When I first investigated the administration of the West Riding after serving in it for ten years, I discovered that in order to maintain the many branches of the service in the County there were some 600 Committees consisting of 9000 members who met approximately 3700 times a year, and the conclusion that I drew was that it was doubtful whether so much voluntary effort was either necessary or wholly rewarding. I doubt very much whether matters have improved now that members are paid more, and corporate management holds sway.

Inevitably there are good and bad Chief Officers in local government, and good and bad Councillors, and there is a major difference between them. The Councillors know that if they have a thoroughly bad member of their staff they can demote him, or if they have the law on their side, dismiss him, or, as a last resort, bring him before the Courts. The Chief Officer has none of these avenues open to him. When dealing with the worst members of his Committee he just has to cope with them as best he can and of course on every Committee there is always one member who is the worst.

It was some time before I realized this. I was fortunate enough to obtain my first administrative post with the City of Birmingham when its Committee standards were as high as any I have known. The Chief Officer at that time was Dr Peter Innes. He took the view that any member of his staff who was given the job of taking a Committee must be able to answer not only those questions which it was thought might be asked, but any others, however remote and unlikely they might be.

But the main force in Birmingham education in those days was the impregnable integrity of the Chairman of its Education Committee, Alderman Byng Kenrick. He was a Conservative, but his relationship with his fellow members of Council was such that he was able to appoint a left-wing idealist as the Chairman of his Higher Education Sub-Committee and a Co-operative Socialist as Chairman of the Elementary Education Sub-Committee, and their morale was such that when they saw eye-to-eye in Committee they voted together in the City Council regardless of their political allegiance. I have never known as unprejudiced and non-political a committee as that presided over by Byng Kenrick in those days. His sheer human quality was such that no one ever had to give a second's thought to the likelihood of his approaching any problem in a way which might be remotely unfair or devious. It therefore came as a shock to me when later on I was forced to realize how rare a person he was. My good fortune was that he set the example which established my values and standards and my debt to him has always been immense. I have often thought in recent years what a splendid example of honest government the Birmingham Education Committee set in those days by comparison with the sordid political wranglings which can so often occur, both centrally and in the localities.

A major lesson that I learned in Birmingham was the importance of the senior clerical staff. An education office normally has a professional administrative staff which consists of the Chief Officer, his Deputy, his Assistant Education Officers, and, on the first rung of the administrative ladder, his Administrative Assistants.

But the office will also be divided into functional sections — primary education, finance, buildings, supplies, further education, and so on, and it is the clerical heads of these sections who form the backbone of the office. They have a thorough and penetrating understanding of the work of their sections.

When I first went to Birmingham all I knew of administration came from my having worked voluntarily for a week or two with Henry Morris, the Director of Education in Cambridgeshire, and from a similar spell with W. H. Perkins in Warwickshire. But it was not until I had a permanent post in Birmingham that I really began to understand how an education office functioned. That I saw so much of the individual sections came about in this way. I was the first Administrative Assistant ever to be employed by the Birmingham Authority and I was doing my first administrative job. It seemed to me at the time that neither the Authority nor I had defined precisely what an Administrative Assistant ought to do. While we were finding the answer to this problem I was able to spend several days in each section of the office in order to find out what was being done and how it was being done. I could not have had a better introduction to my new post. It was then that I learned of the burdens and responsibilities carried by the clerical heads of sections and I still retain two thick books of notes which describe how the Birmingham office worked in those days and pasted inside them are copies of the 150 or so forms which were then in use.

My next move was to go to Cheshire as their first Assistant for Higher Education. F. F. Potter was the Chief Officer and there could not have existed a greater difference in methods used than that between Innes and Potter. Innes, as I have already said, believed that every detail of every matter must be thoroughly understood before that matter was presented to the Committee but he himself rarely attended a Committee, with the effect that when he did so everyone knew that something of weight and importance was afoot. Potter on the other hand attended many meetings. His Committee and its subcommittees met for a whole day each month at an hotel in Crewe and from mid-morning to late afternoon they ploughed through one agenda after another. Potter's attitude and practice was 'Get the stuff out and if anything goes wrong we'll put it right.' Cheshire in those days was very different from the Birmingham I had known. The war was on and I witnessed attitudes and practices that would have been unthinkable in peace time.

But it was when I moved from Cheshire to be the Deputy Education Officer in Worcestershire that I first realized the difference in attitude and practice which can exist between Chief Officers. For example, although there had been Inspectors and organizers in both Birmingham and Cheshire, they were left much to themselves by the Administration. This was not so in Worcestershire where the Education Officer saw a good deal of the schools for which he was responsible and he consulted frequently with his advisory staff about them. The contrasts between Birmingham and Cheshire on the one hand and Worcestershire on the other made me realize that there are Chief Officers whose main interest and concern is for the efficient and tidy administration of their service while others get their main satisfaction from seeing and promoting the achievements of the schools and the quality of the pupils which they produce. Both are important.

When I was appointed as Deputy Education Officer and, within months, as Chief Education Officer of the West Riding, one of the largest Authorities in the country, I had to forget the gentler qualities of Worcestershire and face the tougher facts of the coalfields and wool valleys of Yorkshire.

'As for the Education Officer,' said Alderman Collier when talking of me in full County Council, 'I would not pay him in washers,' and a local meeting in the Calder Valley began by County Councillor Sutcliffe saying, 'I move that the Education Officer be not heard.' My Deputy, Jim Hogan, received the same kind of tribute from County Councillor Ripley, 'Don't take any notice of Hogan, he's paid to talk like that.' We accepted these statements as a regular part of our meetings and my only regret is that I did not record more of them.

Being appointed to a large Authority taught me one firm lesson. I did not have to ponder the matter of delegation, it was inevitable and it had to be on a generous scale. Time and distance made it essential and this was fortunate for me as I did not wish to be over-burdened at the centre; my aim was to get into schools once each week if that was at all possible and I delegated as much of the central office work as I could. The present Education Office of the ILEA quotes a note which I sent to him when we were working together, when I had received some proposals which alarmed me. I wrote, 'I am terrified of this document but I believe you know something about it. Is there something more we ought to know or do? If so will you do it?'

I made it clear to all my senior staff that they all had a job to do; that because of their expertise they could do it, and I did not want to see them unless there were successes or failures of a kind which they believed I should know about. If things in their view were going wrong and I could not suggest ways of putting them right, a group of us would meet to seek solutions. As for committees, I arranged with my Chairman that these should be taken by my senior staff but that anything which he or I thought to be of major importance, together with all major financial matters, should be brought to the newly established Policy and Finance Committee. This meant that my assistant staff gained valuable experience in assuming responsibility for major committees and that as I only attended two committees a month I could find time almost once a week for an exhilarating visit to a school, often in the company of an Adviser who would feel satisfaction in educating me this way and in displaying the quality of schools in his care.

During nearly thirty years as Education Officer of a large Authority I worked with six different Chairmen. Of these the ablest was Alderman Hyman, a powerful and ruthless leader who had great ability but who, although a Socialist, sometimes found difficulty in carrying the South Yorkshire miners with him. He read his agendas meticulously and came to every meeting fully prepared, and once a matter had been approved by his Committee he would fight tooth and nail for it in the Finance Committee and the County Council. He was followed by a Conservative, Alderman Mrs Fitzpatrick, whose approach was somewhat different in that she knew her agendas less well but always insisted on seeing the officer in charge of a committee before the meeting and on going in minute detail into any item on which she had any doubt.

Over the course of this thirty years' span it was inevitable that we should from time to time have to face somewhat sordid difficulties. I was, for instance, always disturbed when rumours went around that certain Unions were paying a retaining fee to certain senior members in order to have their interests watched. Then from time to time attempts would be made to bend the rules in favour of this or that appointment. Normally heads of schools were appointed by four Education Committee members and four local members with a County Council member in the Chair. This meant that the local people only had to win over one County member in order to control the appointment. In order to minimize any unfair pressure I had an agreement with Walter Clayton, the teachers' representative on my Committee, that if he heard of any dubious moves to tamper with an appointment, or if I did, we would consult together in an effort to thwart any unfair intentions. Such appointments did occur from time to time and one of the ironies of my experience is that one of the best head teachers I have ever known was appointed in doubtful circumstances.

On another occasion I had a serious difference of opinion with my Vice-Chairman. I had to advise my Committee to cease to maintain a very small rural grammar school, although his party on the County Council voted to a man to retain it. I accompanied a delegation to see the Secretary of State who supported my view against his own party on the County Council. When this was announced the leader of the political group said to me, 'If you go on as you are doing about that school it will be difficult for me and my backbenchers to establish the friendly relations with you that we had the last time we held office.'

There were continual problems of this kind, but they seldom flared up into importance and as I look back it seems that my jiggery-pokery file was a very small one indeed and much smaller than I suspect that I might be burdened with if I were in office at the present time. There were, as I see it looking back, three main safeguards in my time against dishonesty by members or officials. One was undoubtedly the close relationship to which I have referred between myself and the teachers' representative on the Committee. It was a friendly and helpful association, both of us wanting to maintain high standards and avoid devious procedures. Another was a practice, the significance of which I cannot exaggerate. In the West Riding the party in power held the chairmanship of all committees, but the opposition took each vice-chair. The result of this was that nothing was secretive and it was understood that all information that went to the chairman from an official should also be made known to the vice-chairman. After a lifetime's experience I cannot overstate the value of this practice.

There was one other practice which I adopted which kept us all on the rails. If any member suggested to me any step which seemed at all dubious I would write a note to him asking if he wished me to take the steps he had mentioned and I would then outline his dubious proposal. He then had either to withdraw or face the fact that his proposal was on paper and agreed to by him. These three measures — my association with the teachers' representative, the sharing of the chairmen and vice-chairmen and the committal of dubious proposals to writing, contributed in a major degree to the avoidance of corruption, and promoted an openness and frankness which it seems to me is now lacking in a number of Authorities.

In more recent years committee arrangements have altered considerably. Members are now paid far more than they used to be; the number of committees has increased and in some Authorities political group meetings rank as committees, and members who attend them are paid. There is also less concern than there used to be for Part II of the First Schedule of the Education Act which states that the Authority must consider a report from its Education Committee before exercising any educational function.

Corporate management is the new cult, often occupying valuable time which the Chief Education Officer ought to be giving to the schools and the service generally, and there are now many Authorities which have interposed Personnel or Resource Committees between the Education Committee and the Council. I understand that at worst a relatively trivial appointment, when sought by the head of a school, has to be certified by the Education Officer, counter-signed by his Chairman, considered by the Personnel Officer and approved by a management team, and finally by a management group. As the Chief Education Officer of the ILEA put it,

Corporate Management has struck. Essentially what this means is that many important educational decisions are taken by people who have no knowledge of or direct concern with the education service, and to whom the education service has no direct access.

The wrong handling of a situation is now more overt than it used to be. For instance, only a few days ago I learned of a Medical Officer who was putting himself forward as a political candidate and he explained to those around him that the miners in his constituency relied upon him for a 'note' if they were away from work. The line he openly confessed to taking with them was 'no vote no note', so that his election was assured. I do not think that I ever came across anything uttered so blatantly as this, but apparently it can now happen.

Having made these somewhat dire observations, I ought to make it clear that nothing in my experience would make me wish to replace the democratic nature of local government by any other principle. I would add that the job of Education Officer at all levels can be vastly interesting, especially when it affords insight into national procedures. I well remember my Chairman, Alderman Hyman, placing in my hands documents which he had obviously received from a national source. In 1957 the late Richard Crossman produced a report for a Labour Party study group on schools in the private sector. In it he stated that 'one of the chief characteristics of democracy as distinct from totalitarianism is the freedom it gives to teach and learn outside the state system.' He went on to say:

We believe in the existence of a small private sector, which, if it is not abused, is not only an essential part of democracy, but may well, in so far as it removes centralized uniformity and permits of variety and experiment, have an intrinsic educational value.

There were two main conditions to the continuance of the private sector; one was that the standard should not be allowed to drop below that of the State schools, and the second was that it should not become privileged in a way which would give to the children who were educated within it an unfair advantage in getting into university. Crossman went on in his paper to say that the Party would not interfere with private day schools, other than to ensure their inspection. They would abolish direct-grant schools, allowing them to join the State system or become independent. They would not abolish Independent schools but would ration admissions from them to Oxford and Cambridge Universities, so that these schools would only get their fair share of places by comparison with State schools.

He affirmed that the Party would remove a number of secret subsidies enjoyed by those who used the Independent schools. They would, for instance, declare illegal 'tax rebates on funds provided by industrial firms out of their gross profits for paying for places at Public schools for the sons of their employees.' The final paragraph of Crossman's paper is worthy of full quotation:

We would point out, finally, that the future of this country depends overwhelmingly on rapidly improving the State system of education and ensuring that the best and ablest of our children go through that system along with the others. On the other hand, as democrats, we are determined to avoid any kind of totalitarian coercive measures which threaten the freedom to teach and to learn privately. That right must be maintained, and the suggestions we have made above do, in fact, maintain it. All they do is to ensure that all the funds and energies of our resources will be spent on improving the State system, that none of those funds will, as far as possible, go to subsidizing the private system and that those parents who, after consideration, prefer the private system will pay the full price for doing so.

The most dangerous of these Crossman proposals was couched in these words: 'We propose to abolish fee-paying in the Universities altogether and to insist that entry to Oxford and Cambridge shall in future be by University examination over which the colleges have no control.' This I found most disturbing and I put the following points to my Chairman:

1. Oxford and Cambridge directly or indirectly already influence every Grammar School curriculum in England, but there is some catholicity in the approach to the examining problem by the various Colleges. If you establish a national examination which all children must take in order to get to Oxford and Cambridge, this will in fact completely and utterly dominate every curriculum in the whole of the country. And, what is more, you could not possibly devise a curriculum for which the Public Schools could not more readily prepare than could, say, Mexborough Grammar School. Any such examination could not do other than favour the child from the educationally advantageous home; the English language itself in such a home is a colossal advantage.
2. The examination would be designed to cut out qualities other than intellectual ability, yet you yourself know perfectly well from your experience in interviewing that it is perfectly possible to find a good examinee with nothing else whatever to commend him. Indeed, it is possible to cram a boy with a reasonably good intellect so as to make sure that he will reach the examination standard but at the expense of everything else which goes to make up the sort of youngster that we would like to turn out from our schools.

The point I come to, therefore, is — why do all this when it would only exacerbate these issues? What advantages would you gain by this sort of thing which a quota system would not achieve?

I would have thought that if you do what Crossman suggests in his 8th paragraph, viz line up the Preparatory Schools with the State Junior Schools and then prescribe the subjects, or groups of subjects, in which examinations should take place and then give to the Public Schools a quota of admissions which was generously proportionate to their strength in the country, you would do all that is necessary and could with reasonable safety still leave the job of examining to the Colleges themselves.

My real fear — and it has become almost a phobia with me — is that once you prescribe an entrance examination for Oxford and Cambridge — the energies of every Head and every Assistant in the Grammar Schools of the country will be directed towards circumventing that examination rather than giving the children what they really need, and the schools worst hit would be those schools where the need for cultural activities in the widest sense of that term are most desirable, viz the 'Mexborough Grammar Schools' of the country.

Not all outside contacts were as vital and as interesting as this, but from time to time one met with humour which was very acceptable. I recall the occasion when my Chairman, again Alderman Hyman, wanted support from people of national distinction and he sent a questionnaire to George Bernard Shaw who sent this uncompromising reply, which contains much educational wisdom:

Dear Mr Hyman

Most correspondents are content to ask me for my autograph; and even they don't get it. You ask me for 43 volumes on various aspects of education. You will not get them.

I vehemently deny and repudiate the right of unlimited interferences with the non-adult human being which is assumed throughout the questionnaire. The community has the technical knowledge which is indispensable to civilized life; and some of this — for instance, the multiplication table — does not admit of 'personal happiness in work', and can be sweetened only by the prospect of being given money to spend when it is mastered.

The rest is the child's business, not other people's; but it is the business of the community to see that no child shall lack opportunities of discovering art, literature, music, science, mathematics, etc., in case it should possess faculties that urge it to that sort of employment.

Need I add that I think the questionnaire, as a whole, the most fearful poppycock.

Faithfully
(Signed) G. B. SHAW

Finally I must say that my life has been greatly enriched by the quality of many of the elected members I have had to work with and for. I could write happily about many of them, but one of the first would be Lady Mabel Smith, the daughter of Earl Fitzwilliam. She told me that she was directly descended from Charles II and Nell Gwyn. She was born at Wentworth Woodhouse and I recall visiting this famous building before the Authority took it over as a college of Physical Education. We went into the building and when she arrived at the almost life-size painting of George II she affected to spit because he was a Hanoverian and she was a Stuart. Politically she was a member of the extreme Left and the South Yorkshire miners were devoted to her. She once told me she was the only Stuart Communist who had ever existed. One evening I was due to speak at the school of which she was Chairman of the Governors. I arrived at her house, she opened the door for me and said, 'Do you mind if we come away as soon as you have finished speaking? I have broken my arm in two places today and it is rather painful.' She was eighty-one at the time. It is of course a great joy to any servant of a large concern if those whom he serves and for whom he works are of the quality of Lady Mabel Smith. Unfortunately, but inevitably, in an administration of any size, he is almost certain at the other extreme to have to work at some time or another with officials and councillors who put their own interests first, to the extent that the service becomes dull, sterile and disliked.

These damaging interests may of course be perfectly genuine. There was the time when my committee had just bought a gem of a building, Woolley Hall, near Wakefield. Its effect on people was created to a considerable extent by its magnificent mahogany interior doors which were cherished by those who used the building. A well-heeled councillor with a distinguished Cambridge degree did his best to persuade the governors to make money by removing the mahogany doors, selling them at a high price and replacing them with plywood. But in my experience those who seek quality and the effects which it can produce far outnumber those who care little for such matters.

14

The Pendulum of Education

Inevitably the aims of education vary from generation to generation, and change is brought about in a variety of ways. A government, wishing to solve a difficulty, appoints an advisory committee or a select committee of the House to look into a specific problem, and their solution to it may affect what the Department of Education or the local authorities demand of our schools. In recent decades we have had a multiplicity of such enquiries: Plowden looked at our primary schools, Newsom at the less able half of our teenagers, Robbins at our universities, and there have been many others.

Educational philosophers and professors at our univerities devise new ways of tackling the difficulties of teaching, and their disciples prove the effectiveness or otherwise of the new ideas as they spread into the schools. Teachers such as Montessori or Marion Richardson or Susan Isaacs find new ways of teaching, and the news spreads through the schools, changing both method and curriculum. This happens to a greater or less degree all the time.

More sinister changes are brought about by authoritarian governments who demand that the schools which they provide should support the political or financial actions which they, the governments, decide to take, and even in the more democratic of countries, governments demand that the schools produce more technicians or more scientists or more engineers according to the pressures of the moment rather than that they should do the best for each child according to his needs.

But there is also more natural change which is bound to occur, and indeed it is often as well that it should do so. What inevitably happens is that ways of teaching brought about by tests or by fashion become stale and dull, boring, ineffective and thoughtless. Sensitive and questioning teachers then discover how futile mechanical learning, rote learning, memorization and sheer drill can be at their worst, and these teachers then emphasize the spiritual growth of the child and change to exploratory ways, which create interest and make personal demands on individual children. The results of this individual approach are, at their best, so effective that the new methods become fashionable and are adopted by second-rate teachers who lack understanding of them and allow sentimentalism to invade their teaching. Children then fail to learn as they should, and the cries are 'back to the basics', or 'they are badly behaved', and the schools are charged with neglecting both learning and 'character'.

When we over-emphasize the spirit and personality of the child, the cure is alleged to be more rote learning, more drilled techniques, more obedience and more authority. When we eventually become too rigid, the cure is more self-expression, and more 'finding out'. And so the pendulum swings, and the swinging must be as old as education itself. It swings between mind and spirit, between intellect and personality, between the cognitive and the affective, between obedience and self-realization, between the 'loaves and the hyacinths', between making an atom bomb and deciding whom to kill with it. You choose your antithesis according to your prejudice, or as fashion or the national mood of the moment dictate.

There is no difficulty in tracing this action and reaction through the education service. When the service began, there were schools which were as sensitive and venturesome as anything we can see in our time, but they were few in number.

One of the most remarkable was at Kings Sombourne in Hampshire and one of the first HMIs, the Reverend Moseley, in his report on the school to the Lords of the Treasury makes us realize how much that we pride ourselves on today as advanced teaching method was practised in this village school a quarter of a century before our public service began.

I have set out in the following paragraphs some of our recent innovations but the quotations in italics which follow the paragraph headings are taken from the report which Moseley wrote on Kings Sombourne School in 1847.

In recent years we have done much in our junior schools to relate our scientific teaching to the child's everyday experience.

I began giving the more advanced of the school children short explanations in a common-sense sort of way of the things almost daily passing before their eyes . . . how the pressure of the atmosphere helped them to pump up water, enabled them to amuse themselves with squirts and popguns, to suck up water as they called it through a straw, why the kettle top jumped up when the water was boiling on a fire, why when they wanted to know whether it boiled or not they seized the poker and placing one end on the lid and the other to their ear they knew whether it actually boiled . . . how their clothes are dried and why they feel cold sitting in wet clothes, why on going into school on a cold morning they sometimes see a quantity of water on the glass and why it is on the inside and not on the outside. . .

We today make considerable use of studies of the environment.

In the boys' school they are in the habit of recording in a journal kept by the second master and the senior boys, facts connected with natural history such as the date of the appearance of the first swallow, the first time the song of any particular bird has been heard, the blossoming of different trees, the first ear of wheat or of barley brought to school but growing in the open field and where growing, so as to be able to point out if there was any particular reason as to aspect why that particular field was forwarder than others.

We in our day have discovered, so we believe, that doing is better than being told because we tend to remember what we do and to enjoy it more.

It is sufficient to say that the headmaster's system deals with things rather than with words . . . it is for this reason that thinking and doing are associated in pleasurable relation.

We have concluded in recent years that writing is best stimulated not by exercise but by getting children to write about what they know from experience and we start their history and geography within their familiar locality and then move outwards.

When the child can write sentences on the uses of things familiar to its observation . . . it writes of sheep or cows or horses, wheat, iron or copper, of the village of Kings Sombourne, of the farms and holdings in the parish, or the parish roads or the river Teste which runs through it, of the neighbouring town of Stockbridge, of Hampshire, of the island of Great Britain, of the earth, of the sun, moon and stars.

We have recently invented integrated studies in the belief that such integration will stimulate learning, particularly in the three Rs.

I have certainly never examined little children who could spell so well and that good spelling and good reading and skill in expression of written thoughts go together may be taken as an illustration of the fact that to achieve excellence in any one subject of instruction in an elementary school it is necessary to unite it with others, and that the singular slowness with which the children of our National schools learn to read (a fact to which all our reports have borne testimony) is in some degree to be attributed to the unwise concentration of the labours of the school on that single subject.

We attach importance to the quality of expressive subjects.

Singing is no task to these children, music has found its way into their hearts . . . occasionally the singing classes are assembled in the evening in the classrooms and the singing through the pieces of music they have learned makes a village concert . . .

At the present stage in our development we deplore the fact that parents do not play a significant part in our schools and we claim that things would be better if they were more closely consulted. The Kings Sombourne report states:

We break off a fragment from our own education and give it to the poor man's child in charity...

We consult neither his judgement in the matter nor his independence ... it is the fault of all the eleemosynary [alms-giving] good we seek to do that we claim the right of doing it in our own way ... let us remember that they (the parents) have themselves had no voice in the matter, that in the instruction we offer to their children the springs of opinion among them have never been considered nor their wants consulted...

It is in this that Mr Dawes' [the Headmaster's] success appears to me to lie. He has shown his knowledge of the springs of opinion amongst the poor by consulting their independence and adapted the education he offers them to their wants by a careful study of their condition.

This HMI's report shows us what could and what indeed did happen in a remarkable village school nearly a century and a half ago. In that school at that time the pendulum had moved to an extreme of excellence. What happened at the same time in other schools was that some bad work was revealed and the schools were rightly condemned with the result that in 1870 the government of the day decided to take charge of elementary education and the pendulum swung once more towards formality and rigidity.

A national attitude of the time was revealed by the Vice President of the Privy Council's committee on education, Robert Lowe, who said:

I do not think it is any part of the duty of Government to prescribe what people should learn, except in the case of the very poor whose time is so limited that we must fix upon a few elementary subjects to get anything done at all . . . the lower classes ought to be educated to discharge the duties cast upon them. They should also be educated that they may appreciate and defer to a higher education when they meet it and the higher classes ought to be educated in a very different manner in order that they may exhibit to the lower classes that higher education to which if it were shown to them they would bow down and defer.

It was small wonder when such attitudes could be held that those in authority decided that they must prescribe a curriculum with a common core and insist on methods which would ensure its being observed. And so the 'Code' was established which prescribed doses of measurable knowledge which children could be given in the course of a year. The pupils were grouped not according to age but according to what they knew. Thus children whether six or twelve years of age who could only 'read a short paragraph not confined to words of one syllable' or who could only 'master the multiplication table up to six times twelve' were placed in Standard I and so on up to Standard VII, each grade demanding specifically more than the one which preceded it. Inspectors, reduced to the role of petty examiners, set tests the success in which determined what funds each school should receive from the central government. The Inspectors were given trivial warnings about this. They must not take the same reading book into a school twice and every piece of work submitted by a child must be signed by HMI and dated lest it be submitted twice. Many other similarly primitive details were conveyed as instructions to the Inspectors.

Thus when our service was founded there were few 'hyacinths' and the loaves which were the standard nourishment rapidly became stale. Matthew Arnold, who was an HMI at the time, swung more and more against this soulless routine as it became more deadening. He said of it that 'The circle of the child's reading has been narrowed and impoverished all the year for the sake of the result at the end of it. The teacher is led to think not about his teaching but about managing to hit the requirements.' But the most astonishing thing about the Code was the effect it had on the man who had the major responsibility of supervising its application and maintenance in the later years of its operation. Edmund Holmes was what we should today call the Senior Chief Inspector. It was said of him that 'no living Englishman has had greater opportunities than he of mastering the details of his subject — especially as it is presented in elementary schools.' Having been responsible for supervising the continued imposition of the Code he condemned it utterly and vigorously in a book entitled *What Is and What Might Be*. He described 'what is' as the 'path of mechanical obedience' and 'what might be' as the 'path of self-realization'. The vehemence of his views is still astonishing. These were the opening comments in his preface:

My aim in writing this book is to show that the externalism of the West, the prevalent tendency to pay undue regard to outward and visible 'results' and to neglect what is inward and vital, is the source of most of the defects which vitiate Education in this country. No one knows better than I do that the elementary teachers of this country are the victims of a vicious conception of education which has behind it twenty years of tradition and prescription the malign influence of which was intensified in their case by thirty years or more of Code despotism.

In this preface he also made an astonishing confession about the Code and its function of payment by results which he said 'seems to have been devised for the express purpose of arresting growth and strangling life, which bound us all, myself included, with links of iron and which had many zealous agents of whom I alas! was one.'

In the text of his book Holmes writes sentences such as these:

In nine days out of ten, in nine lessons out of ten, in nine schools out of ten, the teacher is engaged in laying thin films of information on the surface of the child's mind and then after a brief interval in skimming them off in order to satisfy himself that they had been properly laid . . . To be in bondage to a syllabus is a misfortune for a teacher and a misfortune for the school in which he teaches. To be in bondage to a syllabus which is binding on all schools alike is a graver misfortune; to be in bondage to a bad syllabus which is binding on all schools alike is of all misfortunes the greatest.

The point which we who are profoundly concerned with evaluation and assessment and standards ought to bear foremost in mind is that the above quotations and recantations were written by a man who did more to ensure accountability than has ever been done before or since and that he was in the best possible position to judge its effects.

Inevitably there came the swing of the pendulum against the Code. It took the form of what was called heurism or learning by discovery and one of its main advocates was Dr Henry Armstrong FRS, Professor of Chemistry at the London Central Technical College. But long before his time the great politician Edmund Burke had expressed similar views in these terms:

I am convinced that the way of teaching which approaches most nearly the method of investigation is by far the best since not content with serving up a few barren and lifeless truths it tends to set the learner himself on the track of investigation and to direct him into those paths in which the author has made his own discoveries.

In an article published in 1898, 'The Heuristic Method of Teaching, or the Art of making Children discover things for themselves', Dr Henry Armstrong wrote somewhat sentimentally that the whole policy of the teacher's duty 'could be summed up in one little word yet the most expressive in the English language. It is to train them "to do".' He made many suggestions which are well known to those familiar with good primary-school practice of our day.

For example:

When our pupils engage together in work of discovery and are set to find out things for themselves they will naturally be led to discuss their work together, to exchange views, to ask each other's advice. They will be so interested in their work that they will not fail to talk about it. Nothing could be less rational, less truly preparatory for the work of life, than the system of enforced silence we enjoin, but it is a necessary outcome of didactic class teaching. . .

Gradually I would have nearly all classrooms converted into workrooms or work shops . . . teachers would constantly move about noticing what is being done, criticizing and giving brief directions to one group of pupils after another. As it is easy to teach children to use figures to measure and weigh and do simple arithmetic with the aid of a footrule even before they can read or write, such work will have been begun in the Kindergarten class and will in school from the outset take the place of conventional arithmetic.

And one final quotation which is not without its message for our time:

As for apparatus — every effort should be made to utilize ordinary articles, medicine and pickle bottles, jam pots and saucepans and to construct apparatus in the work room. For this latter purpose a carpenter's bench and tools, vice and files and a small lathe, an anvil and even a small forge should wherever possible form part of the equipment. Infinite injury is done at the present day, invaluable opportunities of imparting training are lost by providing everything ready-made.

There was some delay before ideas such as those expressed by Armstrong began to find their way into the teaching of elementary-school children. But they were accepted by HMI; evidence for this is to be found in the first HMI's report ever to be produced for the West Riding Education Committee. In 1905 F. S. Marvin, HMI, wrote the following sentences in an appendix to the Committee's Minutes:

We have not as a nation given sufficient care to the training of our schools in expression, we have forced on reading at a stage in the child's development when it was bound to be a mechanical and deadening process. An obvious and much needed reform in most of our schools is to take several of the hours given weekly to mechanical drill of the younger children in arithmetic and give them to the more sensible training in language, including in this a great deal of oral work in composition and poetry as well as reading and written composition.

The schools are too traditional, too mechanical, too monotonous and the chief fault must rest with those who have enforced a mechanical test of efficiency.

This was powerful support for those who placed less emphasis on the path of mechanical obedience and it encouraged teachers to devote more of their concern to self-realization. But the advent of the 11 plus and two World Wars swung the pendulum back to the 'loaves' and child-centred developments were inhibited for several decades. But by the thirties the pendulum was again beginning to swing towards informality and the Hadow Report of 1931 called for an education based on activity and experience. These early developments caused schools to arise which showed the Plowden Committee in the sixties what was possible. Thus it was that the pendulum swung from the freedom of Kings Sombourne to the rigidity of the Code, from the rigidity of the Code to the freedom of heurism, from the freedom of heurism to the rigidity of the 11 plus and from the rigidity of the 11 plus to the freedom of Hadow and Plowden.

The obvious question we now have to ask is where is the pendulum today, when schools are closing from want of pupils, when we talk easily of a new core curriculum, when the cry is 'back to the basics',when public funds are about to be used to pay for children from LEA schools to be moved into independent schools and when, as Thring put it nearly a century ago, 'There is no peace. Everybody talks. Cabinet ministers lay down the law. Philosophers lay down the law. The very school-boys lay down the law. And the public takes sides with much vehemence.' In these circumstances it is indeed difficult to produce a national educational programme for all the children who need our care. In order to see more clearly into the problems which beset us, I asked some former colleagues of mine to set down some of the questions which are causing them concern. I have set out at random some of these questions, as they form a poignant criticism of the condition of our education service as it is today.

Do the politicians of the Right intend by means of the assisted places scheme to rob our local authority schools of their bright pupils in order to strengthen our Independent schools? If so, shall we not rob the poor to help the rich?

Do our politicians of the Left intend to abolish our Independent schools in order, as they see it, to strengthen local authority schools and eventually to shape our society to their beliefs?

Will our politicians and councillors, looking for money, insist on finding it by cutting down on the maintenance, cleaning and re-decorating of their schools, and if so, will they not create children who 'don't care'?

Will a core curriculum improve standards, or is the real intention to devise a means of comparing school with school and teacher with teacher?

In times of harsh economy, is there not a danger that we reduce and even denounce as frills some of our most civilizing school activities such as art, crafts, music and adventure training?

In our search for the examinable and the measurable, is there not a danger that we merely concentrate on the techniques and even on the tricks of teaching?

If more is to be done by machines and less by men and women, are the curricula that we now follow giving to our children the preparation for life which they will need?

When we changed from the School Certificate to the GCE, were we wrong to abandon compulsion in such subjects as English, maths and science?

Do we as a nation tend to look down on those who are below average ability, and who cannot pass examinations? If so, what dangerous kind of adults may our children grow into?

Will possible economies in school transport reduce the demand for education in church schools, and is this what we intend?

Are we placing our pre-school units where the need for them is greatest or where the middle class demand for them is most persuasive?

In dealing with potentially anti-social children, should we not concentrate more on prevention and less on cure and punishment?

Does the education we provide deal adequately with the fact that children born into our most harsh social and industrial areas often face difficulties of speech, expectation and home experience which severely handicap their educational progress?

Is it a fact that in pay and resources we favour the teachers who teach the gifted and the older pupils, and provide less well for those who have the harder task of teaching and caring for the slow?

Are we unwisely pressing too many of our adolescents into academic higher education to the detriment of our technical and manual skills?

Is the staffing in some areas of higher education more generous than we can afford?

This list could of course be vastly increased, but I will conclude it with the view expressed by HMI Moseley in his report to the Lords of the Treasury on Kings Sombourne School in 1847. He expresses an ideal not yet reached.

Education is not a privilege to be graduated according to man's social condition, but the right of all, in as much as it is necessary to the growth of every man's understanding; and into whatsoever state of life it may please God to call him, an essential element of his moral being.

15

The Background: One Hundred Years of Education

The way we now organize our schools, what we teach in them and how we teach it, owes much to what we did in the first hundred years of our public education service from 1870 to 1970. I have therefore decided to include as my last chapter parts of a lecture which at the invitation of the Department of Education and Science I gave in the Central Hall Westminster in May 1970. The occasion was to commemorate a century of state education in this country. The subject was a vast one and to tackle it within the time available I decided to concentrate on the three great Acts of 1870, 1902 and 1944 and to consider in respect of each Act what we set out to do, what opposition had to be overcome in order to do it, and whether the results were good.

In the Act of 1870 we set out to establish a national system of elementary schools in which the children of the labouring poor, that is of parents who could not afford 9d a week in fees, should be taught. After all, this was something which most countries of the Western world had done years earlier.

But when we put the question: What resistance had to be overcome? — we find that the opposition was immense. The working classes were on the whole apathetic. But there were those whom Matthew Arnold called the 'selfish vulgar of the upper classes' and they believed that the 'less a poor man learned except his handicraft the better' and that 'to educate the poor was like putting the torch of knowledge into the hands of rick burners'. And of course there were the churches. They for the most part had done the job of teaching for hundreds of years and they felt strongly that they should continue to do it. 'Why', as Lord Stanley put it, 'should there be an incursion by the civil power into spiritual matters?' But it was the non-conformists who were the militants. They bitterly resented the idea of more public money being spent on church schools. What they wanted was free compulsory rate-supported non-denominational elementary schooling, and they formed in Birmingham a pressure group called the Education League. The way this league was founded and the way it operated was a measure of the intensity of non-conformist feeling in the country. To all who have an allegiance to Birmingham, the names of those on the first subscription list are fascinating. It was led by George Dixon and included, amongst others, one Beale, one Martineau, one Chance, one Nettlefold, two Chamberlains and four Kenricks. All these men but one backed their views with a contribution of either £500 or £1000 and within four months of its foundation the League had £60,000 at its disposal, it had organized 200 public meetings, issued a quarter of a million publications, started a monthly paper with a circulation of 20,000 and had organized branches in all the major cities of the country.

It was amidst this passion and conflict that Gladstone's government introduced the bill in February 1870 and he called upon the Member for Bradford, W. E. Forster, a Quaker and the son-in-law of Thomas Arnold of Rugby, to do it. The opposition was fierce and there is little doubt that Forster had to trim his intentions, indeed at one stage, according to Matthew Arnold, Gladstone virtually took the bill into his own hands. One religious amendment alone was debated for four nights running and on another one-third of the government supporters walked out. When the bill was finally passed in August and Forster went back to Bradford to receive a motion of acclaim from his supporters it was an amendment deploring the Act which was carried.

So much for the intentions of the bill and the resistance to it, but was the result good? We had made a start, but the education which the Act was to provide was not free, it was not compulsory, it was not secular and it was not entirely rate-supported. There were in fact two systems, the one consisting of State-aided church schools and the other of rate-supported board schools.

But it might be held against the 1870 Act that one of its worst failings was to do nothing at all to curb the effect of that pernicious system which we all know as payment by results, introduced in the early 1860s. I am bound to dwell on this because it lasted for over thirty-five years and it has, I believe, left its corrupting mark on us to this day in that we still use external examinations because we do not trust our teachers, we still concentrate on facts rather than values, on memory rather than understanding, and on what can be measured to the neglect of what cannot. In 1861 the Newcastle commission had recommended that grants should only be paid to schools 'after a searching examination by a competent authority of every child in the school'. The idea was taken up and enforced by the then Vice President of the Privy Council's education committee, Robert Lowe, of whom Professor Asa Briggs has said that he set out the most comprehensive case against democracy in the nineteenth century.

He it was who having failed to thwart the extension of the franchise in 1867 said with bitter irony, 'We must educate our masters' and who also said, this time without irony, that the lower classes ought to be educated to discharge the duties cast upon them and to bow down and defer to a higher cultivation when they met it. What children had to learn was set out in the standards of a Code and the school received a grant only for those children who passed a test set and marked by HMI and appropriate to the standards they were working at, at the time.

Initially the tests were set in the three Rs only so that all other subjects tended to be neglected, as did those pupils who had no chance of passing the test.

When I first learned of this baneful device I used to wonder what a compassionate HMI would do if he came across a school which was the only glimmer of light in a dismal area but whose pupils could not hope to pass because of the poverty of the start they got at home. Would he fail the children, stop the grant and so close the school, or was there some other way? The answer came to me a year or two ago in a letter from an uncle of my wife, then 87 years of age. He was himself the son of a Durham miner and the father of a distinguished space scientist. He knew nothing of Robert Lowe or of payment by results but this is what he wrote of his village school at Escomb in County Durham, as it was some ninety years ago just before payment by results came to an end.

There was a system of inspection in the elementary schools in my day. I understand that this was under the aegis of government appointed Inspectors who carried out the inspection. They used the card system. On printed cards they arranged a series of problems in various subjects for different standards. At exam times these were handed out to the pupils to be solved. In some way the schoolmasters would get possession of these cards in advance of the exams. By exchange of information they could work on the answers along with scholars to be examined so they usually passed the exam. I remember working out answers to test cards which usually turned up on examination days. In after years I thought that some of the Inspectors themselves were well aware of these practices.

And so our verdict on the Act of 1870 must be that we made a start, and we made it against fierce opposition, but the classroom education which emerged was often mean, meagre and mechanical.

What happened between the first two Acts? Payment by results continued until 1897. It was government arithmetic which earned the grant and stirring sentences such as 'It is not a sin to sit on a sod and nod' were read from the Inspectors' cards. But pressures from the Birmingham League and from mounting public opinion ensured that schooling was first made compulsory and eventually free. Numbers in the schools rose from one to six million and the average school life increased from two-and-a-half to seven years. All this represented a massive achievement and it gave rise to a demand for secondary schools which was met by adding senior tops to elementary schools. And so when we come to ask what were the intentions of the Act of 1902 we find that these were to create local education authorities which would fuse the church and board schools into one system, and to build and maintain secondary schools.

What was the resistance which had to be overcome? It is difficult for us to imagine the passions which built up in the last decades of the last century about the spending of public money on church schools. It was obvious to everybody that without financial help the church schools just could not continue to exist, but for some reason or other the idea of giving them rate aid was far more abhorrent to their opponents than giving them State aid, which after all had been done albeit reluctantly by some for seventy years. The result was that when in 1896 Sir John Gorst tried to introduce a bill which would help church schools from the rates there was a national uproar. The outcry against the religious sections of it was so immediate, so intense and so sustained that it was withdrawn and the Duke of Devonshire is reputed to have gone up to Sir John's room and said, 'Gorst, your damned Bill's dead.'

Then a crisis was precipitated. All over the country and with the connivance and indeed the support of the Department, School Boards had been adding senior tops to their elementary schools to meet the new demand for secondary education which universal elementary education had created. Moreover the new County Councils had been allowed to spend excise money, whisky money as it was called, on technical and manual instruction. The problem which now arose was which of these two bodies, the School Boards or the County Councils, were going to be allowed to develop secondary schools.

In London this grew into an overt quarrel between the London School Board and the London County Council and the very able Robert Morant, who had been chosen over the head of his chief, Michael Sadler, to prepare a new bill, decided to settle the matter once and for all by calling in the Auditor, Mr Barclay Cockerton, who promptly surcharged three of the School Board members for specific sums paid out for drawing instruction and for science. The case went to appeal as The Queen v Cockerton in the Queen's Bench Division of the High Court. Mr Justice Kennedy said, 'If the elements of drawing or of chemistry are beyond the limits of elementary education then the rate payers are entitled to say that these subjects shall not be taught.' In his summing up Mr Justice Wills said that for the Boards to teach subjects of this kind was the *ne plus ultra* of extravagance and the auditor won his case.

As higher grade schools had been going up all over the country with the support of the Education Department the decision caused general panic and a holding bill was rushed through in 1901 to legalize what had already been done.

The debate on the bill lasted from 16 October to 11 November when the guillotine was applied. On one night between 11 p.m. and 3 a.m. there were no fewer than twenty-two divisions. Arthur Balfour said that in the course of his life he had never known so many amendments to a bill and that the problem was far less easy to solve than the South Africa problem. Dr Clifford, the leading Baptist Minister of the day, whom I remember meeting when I was very small, led the non-conformist revolt. He said there were 16,410 head teacher departments in English church schools, schools kept going in salaries and books and wear and tear, in nearly everything, by the rate and tax payers and from all these, free churchmen, because they were free churchmen, were excluded, and his pamphlet against the bill had a phenomenal sale. Correspondence in the press was long and sustained. One letter alone in *The Times* from Sir William Harcourt ran to over 6000 words. A young politician, David Lloyd George, who was in the thick of the trouble, had found a report by an Inspector who admitted that he always questioned dissenters' children on the church catechism, adding, 'Thus in fact we are training non-conformist children to be children of the church,' and this put the fat well and truly in the fire. Lloyd George said that if the bill became an Act the clergyman would come down to the school like a roaring lion seeking what little non-conformists he could devour at the expense of the rate payer and that the bill would rivet a clerical chain round the neck of the people. There were protest meetings all over the country, the biggest was presided over by Lord Rosebery in the Queen's Hall in June. The attendance was so great that there had to be an overflow meeting. The speakers were all eminent men and women and again Lloyd George said of the bill that it was originated by a wily Tory Cardinal, promoted by state clergy, who accepted Protestant pay for propagating Catholic doctrines and added its advocacy was the last act of treachery in the career of one who had sold many of his principles. The Welsh counties, led by Glamorgan, said that if the bill became an Act they would not operate it and for a time they did not.

We in the West Riding did not behave like these insurgent Welshmen; we were much more reasonable. It is true that Alderman Willy Clough wrote to the *Yorkshire Post* about the dilapidated denominational school houses whose vitiated clericalized atmosphere was deadly alike to body and soul, but this merely meant that he did not much care for church schools. We did not say we would not administer the Act. What we did say was, and I quote County Councillor S. Wood, 'We propose to administer the Education Act insofar as we think it wise, and to leave the administration of those portions of the Act that we think are not wise. This is not violating the law, it is simply not carrying it out.' And we pursued this very reasonable policy in the West Riding. We thought that it was not wise to pay the teachers for the time they spent on denominational teaching so we deducted £1,126. 17s. 0d from their combined salaries. A case was brought against us which was taken up to the House of Lords on appeal before we finally lost it. The same thing happened to us when we prosecuted a parent for taking his child out of school on Ascension Day, but we did manage to pay 3s. 9d per child less for voluntary-school teachers than for teachers in council schools.

At this time thousands of people up and down the country, including both my grandfather and my father, refused point blank to pay the local rate and their property was distrained.

Now how did all this passion subside? My grandfather was at the time the village schoolmaster in the village of Eastcombe in Gloucestershire and this is what he wrote to my father in September of 1903:

My dear Son,

I gave a holiday yesterday morning and Mama and I strolled over the hills to Stroud. We managed to get a seat just behind the door and then every seat was occupied. Most of our party that came after had to stand or sit cramped. Some sat on each other's knees. Orders were then given to admit no more. For four hours we sat, before our cases were called, and then each one was dismissed with two or three questions. I was one of the last. After the usual legal questions were asked came the question to me, 'Why have you not paid the rate?' I replied 'I have offered on two occasions to pay a part of the rate.' Then he was cutting me short with the question about the conscientious objection, etc., when I thought I would express a thought that had come into mind, in reference to the absurdity of calling it a 'poor' rate. 'Allow me to say, Sir, that I am summoned here for the non payment of the *poor* rate, if it were merely a question of the *poor* rate, I should have been willing to pay, if it had been twice as much, but when a gentleman with an income of £15,000 poses before the country as a poor man, and demands to come upon the rates for the teaching of his particular doctrines in the schools it is time make a stand.' The magistrate, 'How much will you pay?' All except 1s. 3d I answer. Distraint order for 1s. 3d was then made against me.

This is a strange world, but Jesus reigns.

All our love to you all.

Your Father

So much for the resistance that had to be overcome, and now for the third question, was the result a good one? It was still not possible for church schools to obtain public monies for building purposes though the local authorities could now spend rates on their maintenance. And of course new secondary schools were built and these new schools did not set out with the stigma of the poor rate on them. They inherited their ethos from the old established grammar schools and some at least were fired by a new and independent idealism drawn from men like Ruskin and William Morris. Many of the 1902 schools were fine in many ways. In my own county, the West Riding, two of them produced Henry Moore and Sir John Cockcroft, and this is no mean achievement.

And so of the 1902 Act we may say that it did what it set out to do, the immense resistance to it was overcome and almost immediately the resultant secondary education was good.

What happened between 1902 and 1944? At the end of World War I we put the leaving age up to fourteen, made nursery schools possible and promised ourselves day continuation schools, a promise we never redeemed. It was not until the twenties that we ceased to organize in standards, and a decade later it was still possible for George Formby to raise a laugh from his music hall audience by saying that he left school from Standard III.

But things began to move. R. H. Tawney inspired us with the idea of secondary education for all, and the NUT started to express a preference for what they then called multi-bias schools. The Hadow Committee divided the all-age school into junior and senior schools. The senior school had to have a span of at least three years, so three was subtracted from the leaving age of fourteen and the mystic age of 11 plus was born.

In 1932 those of us who came from colleges and universities, as I did, could not get jobs and the May Committee were so appalled at our national extravagance that they wrote, 'The education provided by the state is sometimes superior to that provided for the children of middle class parents.' There were more and more scholarships and free places and we established secondary, technical, commercial, art and selective central schools. Sir Cyril Norwood, in succession head of

Bristol, Marlborough, and Harrow, led a committee in 1943 which said virtually that children were born into three categories — those who loved learning, those who wanted to apply it and those who dealt with concrete things, and we believed it and called them grammar, technical and modern school children. During these years the ruts cut by the routines of the external examinations grew deeper and to them was added the new fangled device of the intelligence test. We were back to Thomas Gradgrind who saw boys and girls as pitchers to be filled full of facts and 'who with a rule and a pair of scales was ready to weigh and measure any parcel of human nature and tell you exactly what it came to.'

Then we had another war and towards the end of it the 1944 Act. What were the intentions of this great Act? The main ones were to make capital monies available for church school building, to settle what remained of the religious problem by the device of aided, controlled and special agreement schools, to get rid of Part III Authorities which dealt only with elementary schools, to put all secondary schools under a common code of regulations, to raise the school leaving age, to establish nursery schools and county colleges for youngsters released from industry and to inspect Independent schools. On one controversial subject the White Paper which preceded the bill said, 'There is nothing in favour of a system which subjects children at the age of 11 to the strain of a competitive examination.' But the main achievement of the 1944 Act was that for the first time in our history we had a national system of primary, secondary and further education controlled and not merely supervised by a Minister of the Crown and designed to contribute to the spiritual, moral, mental and physical well-being of our people. It was a noble conception which will for all time be associated with the name of R. A. Butler.

When we come to ask what obstacles had to be overcome in order to pass the 1944 Act, we are bound to admit that though they no doubt seemed considerable at the time they were as nothing compared with the fury and turmoil of 1870 and 1902.

I propose in conclusion to apply my third question, 'Was the result good?' to the Butler Act and to apply it not only to the administrative clauses but to the grand purpose of that Act, for whether or not this purpose is fulfilled will I believe do much to determine our future happiness and success as a nation.

As far as the main administrative intentions go we have done well. It is true that we have not established county colleges and that ever since the last war because of the increase in births our nursery schools have been filled with children of school age. But we raised the school leaving age and we are going to do it again, we abolished Part III Authorities, we unified the system and we made public monies available for church school buildings. And educationally we have also made progress for which we can take credit. We have paused to ask what we are doing and why we are doing it and what we ought to be doing that is even better, and Crowther, Newsom and Plowden have given us the answers. And we have done great things for our abler pupils. We have broadened the old School Certificate track which now leads to 'O' and 'A' level and we shall double it again in the next ten years, and we are prepared to pay more to educate the really afflicted child than it would cost us to send him to Eton.

But what about the grand purpose of the Act, and by this I mean the intention expressed by such phrases as 'secondary education for all', 'parity of esteem', 'education according to age, ability, aptitudes', and the 'spiritual, moral, mental and physical well-being of the community', phrases which occurred sometimes in the Act, sometimes in the supporting documents. If these phrases meant anything at all they meant in simple terms that we should get the best out of every child and in so doing we should raise the whole level of our people and not merely erect a ladder from the gutter to the university, as Huxley once put it. They also meant, I think, that the care and concern that we bestow on our children should match their need for such care.

And although they did not say so specifically, I think those who framed the Act would have agreed with a view put forward by the visionaries of the last century, men like Kay Shuttleworth and Arnold, when they first saw state education on the horizon and saw it 'as a civilizing agent even more than as an instructing agent'.

Now whether this view was really endorsed by public opinion a century ago I do not know, neither, as I have said, do I know whether those who framed the Act of 1944 would have endorsed it, though I suspect they might. What I do know is that we obviously do not endorse it, it is totally alien both to our practice and to our national attitude. We have either consciously or by default framed a secondary education system which we all know to be graduated according to men's social condition; our very nomenclature 'public', direct-grant' and 'maintained', bespeaks these gradations. And though the gradations are neither endorsed nor forbidden by the Act I find it very difficult to see how their existence can contribute to the spiritual and moral well-being of our community, which is one of the noble purposes of the Act.

For as long as we have provided secondary education we have been ruthlessly selective. Our famous public schools, so often founded for the poor, have become highly selective schools for the rich, and those schools which receive their grant direct from the Secretary of State are so selective that they draw one-quarter of their pupils from the top 2½ per cent of the ability range, one-third from the families of managers and professionals, and only 8 per cent from semi-skilled and unskilled homes. This national attitude is reflected in the schools themselves. The public and direct-grant schools publish their Oxbridge league table, the grammar schools report their university successes and the modern schools tell us of their 'O' levels. We select at eleven, at sixteen and at eighteen, and every time we select we discard or undervalue those left behind. Our national attitude has been and still is, 'Suffer little children with an IQ of 120+ to receive the best secondary education for they shall add most to the gross national product.' And this attitude can prevail just as much within one school as it does from school to school. To those who think I am overstating this case let me recall what we do to John Robinson.

When the Newsom Committee was studying the problems of youngsters of average and below average ability it divided them into three groups — the top ability group John Brown, the middle two ability groups John Jones, and those in the least able quarter John Robinson, and it conducted a detailed statistical survey in order to find out what happened to the youngsters from these ability groups. Let me give you a description of John Robinson based on what we found out about him.

He is the son of an unskilled worker with a large family, living in a poor area. He starts at his secondary school below average in height, weight and measurable intelligence and is placed in a low stream in the school. It is he who would profit most by a generous use of the school's practical rooms but he is in fact allowed less use of them than either John Brown or John Jones.

Though teaching him is one of the hardest jobs he is often taught by the poorest teachers and when a teacher is absent it is he who has to make shift. The school is not concerned about him as it is about those who will bring to it the renown of examination successes. He is not worth home-work and when given it he often doesn't do it. He dislikes wearing uniform and is seldom a member of a school society or team. He has free dinners and although Newsom did not point this out he often has to queue for his ticket after the fee-payers have received theirs. He who most needs the spur of success rarely experiences it. He lacks that most powerful of all educational forces, the parental aspiration which does so much for the middle-class child, and he lacks what HMI described 100 years ago as 'that recognition which our natures crave and acknowledge with renewed endeavour'.

And now may I continue where Newsom left off. He leaves school as soon as he can but is often amongst the last to land a job and when he does land one it does not carry the distinction of day release or an apprenticeship, and of course as he has been virtually discarded by his school he avoids the youth club and further education, both of which remind him of it. He knows the misery of unimportance and as no teacher has ever been a John Robinson no teacher knows the depth of his resentment. I suspect also that his achievement diminishes in relation to his measured ability as he passes through the school even more than is the case with John Brown and John Jones.

Now we have a bad conscience about John Robinson as indeed they have in the United States where more often than not he is coloured. There they are desegregating by mixing coloured and whites, here we are desegregating by mixing the slow and the bright. The comprehensive school is a sop to our conscience but it is the worst place of all in which to place John Robinson if it happens to be a school in which the concern of the staff for their pupils diminishes as the streams get lower. And we delude ourselves if we think that we can easily change a national attitude by an organizational device. 'Look how the place has gone down since the moderns came in' is how one teacher put it. 'If you come to school with dirty hair like that again my girl we shall send you over to the modern school where there are lots more like you' was what a senior mistress said to a motherless fifteen-year-old who was as indifferent to her father as he to her. No amount of organization will change attitudes of this kind. We need a change of heart such as occurred when we ceased to laugh at lunatics or when we came to believe a hundred years ago that the children of the labouring poor might after all be taught. It would of course help if we thought a little more carefully about the way we still pay by results. Money and prestige go to the teachers who have the easy job of imparting someone else's syllabus to children, many of whom cannot fail to learn, while those who successfully meet the difficult challenge of the dull mind go unrewarded and unrecognized.

There will be those who will say that this is all very touching but after all there have always been the John Robinsons of this world, and this of course is true. But I suspect that things are beginning to happen to him now which have not happened before. He has seldom, for instance, been so conspicuous. Sixty years ago when one child in ten went to the grammar school and the nine others thought him 'stuck up' and called after him in the street these nine were not really upset, they after all made up the vast majority and there were other ways of getting on than by going to the grammar school. But now, as more and more go on to some form of higher education, those who obviously fail are bound to be far more conscious of their failure and, as one United States Senator put it, they 'harbour a deep fury against the schools that have failed them'. Moreover, as unskilled jobs diminish and skilled jobs increase the John Robinsons of this world will be more and more conspicuously forced into a minority group of school failures who will later on be still further embittered by the fact that they are not only unemployed but unemployable. And things are likely to get worse rather than better as we spend more and more on the claimants for higher education who will flood from our sixth forms in the next ten years. We ought perhaps to pause more often to consider our priorities. I suspect for instance that the amount that we spend providing one vet with a second degree would enable us to keep a nursery school of 70 to 100 children open for one year.

This may be too heavy a price to pay for the fashion of higher degrees and perhaps we ought to spend more on the John Robinsons and perhaps we shall run into very severe trouble if we do not! Already there is trouble with our slower learners in the fourth years of some of our schools, mainly because we do not care about them and we do not know how to teach them, and they know and resent the fact that the schools are failing them. I suspect, furthermore, that this trouble may become dangerously ugly in some schools when we raise the school leaving age, and stupid unthinking people will attribute it to slackness in authority and indiscipline.

If we cannot find it in our hearts to care about John Robinson and get the best out of him we ought at least to ponder the possible results of our attitude. The police now patrol the high schools in some cities of the USA, and lest anyone say this could not happen here let him bear in mind that crimes of violence amongst older adolescents have increased by just under 1000 per cent in the last eighteen years, though it is true that amongst youngsters of fourteen to seventeen the increase has only been 758 per cent.

There is however hope. I believe that the schools could lead rather than follow society in bringing about a change of attitude and that many junior schools are doing just this. In the best of these schools learning has became an exciting and happy business with the children themselves bearing much responsibility for what they do. The newer ways of learning force the teacher's attention on the individual and none is lost in the crowd.

The next ten years will tell us whether the same thing can happen in our secondary schools, whether they are really to fulfil the great purpose of the 1944 Act by getting the best out of every child or whether we are to pull society asunder still further by plying the quick with privilege and money to the ever continuing sacrifice of the slow.

There are I think more hopeful signs in our secondary schools now than there were in the primary schools in the early fifties. There are schools where success is made to reach everyone, where responsibility is borne by those who need to bear it, as well as by those able to do so, schools where there are pupils' councils discharging responsibilities rather than prefects performing set duties, schools where the more gifted offer compassionate help to those who are frail, schools which make social education an important part of their task and in which all children are led by sympathetic guidance to a better knowledge of themselves.

But there are also strong forces pulling in the opposite direction. There is still the national habit of drawing examination lines and under-valuing those who fall beneath them, there are the external examinations themselves which relieve the teacher of thought about why he is teaching what he is teaching to any individual child, and which make him see his job as a pearl-casting process, there is the habit in many schools of claiming credit for their successes and blaming their failures on the child or on the Almighty, and there is the growth of divorce and illegitimacy and of other forms of adult selfishness.

And so our judgement of whether we have done our best with the 1944 Act and whether the result is a good one must, I suggest, be suspended for another five to ten years. The possibility of making it good is still with us. It would be wrong of me to pretend I am not fearful about our attitude to our slow learners in this rapidly changing society. We are not getting the best out of them, we care too little for them and we are unaware of the risks we are running.

Edward Thring saw all this very clearly. He said that the pride of intellect was to be unchained and there was to be no place for the weak. The abuse and glorification of intellectual strength was, in his view, the vandal over again but in a new guise and might produce similar results. These are three sentences taken from his chapter on the theory of teaching, written some ninety years ago:

The appeal to success, Prizes and Prize-winning, bids fair to be the watchword of the day. But what does this do for the majority, for the non-competing crowd who nevertheless do not politely die off and make room and cannot, through modern squeamishness, be killed off and buried?'

The weak are pushed into a corner and neglected, their natural tendency to shrink from labour is educated into despair by their being constantly reminded, directly or indirectly, that their labour is no good.

And so in conclusion I must voice my anxiety about our interpretation of the 1944 Act. Secondary education for all must be what adult society wills it to be and if the only challenge we can offer the young is that of material prosperity, if we over-value the quick who can add to it and discard the slow who cannot, the former will despise our values and the latter resent our indifference and we shall blame both for what is our failing. And there will be much bitterness and much discord in our society.

The weak will always be with us and as Thring said, 'It is an axiom that a system which takes no count of the weak is no part of God's true world. Gather up the fragments that remain that nothing be lost.'

The choice is ours.

Index